# Microsoft Dynamics CRM API Development for Online and On-Premise Environments

**Mark Beckner**
**Triston Arisawa**

Microsoft Dynamics CRM API Development for Online and On-Premise Environments

Copyright © 2013 by Mark Beckner and Triston Arisawa

ISBN-13 (pbk): 978-1-4302-6346-3

ISBN-13 (electronic): 978-1-4302-6348-7

President and Publisher: Paul Manning
Lead Editor: Steve Weiss
Editorial Board: Steve Anglin, Mark Beckner, Ewan Buckingham, Gary Cornell, Louise Corrigan, Morgan Ertel, Jonathan Gennick, Jonathan Hassell, Robert Hutchinson, Michelle Lowman, James Markham, Matthew Moodie, Jeff Olson, Jeffrey Pepper, Douglas Pundick, Ben Renow-Clarke, Dominic Shakeshaft, Gwenan Spearing, Matt Wade, Tom Welsh
Coordinating Editor: Christine Ricketts
Copy Editor: Corbin Collins
Compositor: SPi Global
Indexer: SPi Global
Artist: SPi Global
Cover Designer: Anna Ishchenko

Distributed to the book trade worldwide by Springer Science+Business Media New York, 233 Spring Street, 6th Floor, New York, NY 10013. Phone 1-800-SPRINGER, fax (201) 348-4505, e-mail orders-ny@springer-sbm.com, or visit www.springeronline.com. Apress Media, LLC is a California LLC and the sole member (owner) is Springer Science + Business Media Finance Inc (SSBM Finance Inc). SSBM Finance Inc is a Delaware corporation.

For information on translations, please e-mail rights@apress.com, or visit www.apress.com.

Apress and friends of ED books may be purchased in bulk for academic, corporate, or promotional use. eBook versions and licenses are also available for most titles. For more information, reference our Special Bulk Sales–eBook Licensing web page at www.apress.com/bulk-sales.

Any source code or other supplementary materials referenced by the author in this text is available to readers at www.apress.com. For detailed information about how to locate your book's source code, go to www.apress.com/source-code/.

# Contents at a Glance

# Contents

# Foreword

I have had the pleasure to work with Dynamics CRM since its 1.1 version. I can be honest—I didn't feel cheated when Microsoft skipped the 2.0 release, and although it has been a late bloomer in the CRM market, it has gained significant traction over the last few releases and manages to land in the right (top right, to be specific) quadrant according to Gartner year after year.

Software, like clothing, seems to have trends, and CRM has been subject to these software fashion trends. CRM software is fashionable again, and innovation in social media, cloud computing, big data, and mobility have all provided a renewed focus for Microsoft to innovate with Dynamics CRM. Product release cycles are shrinking, and deployment is becoming faster. At the same time, customization and integration of systems are becoming easier. Mobile applications are making it easier to access information and mine data analytics, and business intelligence is making it easier to gain better business insights. Marketing automation software is another category that has emerged rapidly as part of the expanded CRM offering. Vendors are integrating their data with CRM software to provide a deeper level of customer insight. Future versions of CRM will have a richer feature base for marketing automation.

It's now easy to purchase and own CRM through an Office 365 subscription and even easier to integrate it with all the familiar tools, like SharePoint, Outlook, and Lync. This creates a connected and powerful user experience that only Microsoft is able to provide. Through Microsoft's cloud offering, partner-hosted and on-premise model Microsoft Dynamics is available to organizations on their specific terms. In addition to being an effective sales, marketing, and service automation solution, Dynamics CRM is a powerful platform that allows you to orchestrate and automate business processes.

System ownership costs are accrued in the form of infrastructure costs, software use rights, implementation and customization, training, support, and maintenance. As CRM consultants and architects, we spend most of our time helping organizations implement, integrate, and extend Dynamics CRM's capabilities. Dynamics CRM provides a rich set of tools and features for any organization to customize its system. It is a .NET-based enterprise application with an n-tier architecture. Complex software components make up this platform, including a database, a web services layer for integration, workflows for business process automation, forms and dialogs for data entry, and a reporting infrastructure for business insight.

For a successful CRM implementation, I suggest the following guidelines:

- Invest in the partner selection that allows you to have a combination of good functional skills (preferably experience with your industry) and technical skills bundled with methodologies and reusable assets.

- Establish a good delivery model through a set of onsite, offsite, or hybrid teams.

- Ensure the partner follows a defined delivery methodology, like Sure Step, and uses a decision analysis framework.

- Have reusable technical assets, tools, add-ons, and a network of other partners.

- Determine the parts of projects that you want to outsource or offshore like development, maintenance, and administration.

- Strike a balance between cost and reward so you get the most of your investment.

As a Microsoft partner, IOTap performs various activities, including planning, estimation, design, development, training, administration, and support. Partner selection is a critical step that happens early in the process. A wide range of consulting skills are available with an equally wide range of consulting bill rates. There are partners with CRM solutions for an industry, functional and technical experts, and administrators, and all these are available through different models now—as onsite consultants, offsite consultants, and even through firms like ours that offer hybrid models.

Over the last ten years we have supported some of the best CRM partners and customers and have been involved in all aspects of CRM implementations across practically every industry. There are key phases of a CRM implementation that require an intimate conversation and understanding about the business and its processes.

Whether you work for a Dynamics CRM partner or within the Shared Services group of an organization, the opportunity for what you can do with it is growing. It is precisely with this thought and the capability of the platform that CRM partners like us are adding solutions and building add-ons and plugins to explore a whole new market opportunity. With CRM 2013 around the corner, Microsoft is now making it even easier for customers to pick and choose the level of functionality to pay for. This creates an even more compelling reason to understand the platform's capabilities and create enhancements using the SDK and development techniques to extend and integrate CRM.

As a Microsoft Partner I was delighted to get this opportunity to contribute to this book. I have worked with Mark Beckner on numerous occasions and in different capacities as a partner, customer, and vendor. In every capacity Mark has always been able to take a complex problem and present a solution with ease and simplicity. I am sure you will receive that same value from this book.

Ismail Nalwala

Principal

IOTAP

inalwala@IOTAP.com

# About the Authors

**Mark Beckner** is a technical consultant specializing in business strategy and enterprise application integration. He runs his own consulting firm, Inotek Consulting Group, LLC, delivering innovative solutions to large corporations and small businesses. His projects have included engagements with numerous clients throughout the U.S. and range in nature from mobile application development to complete integration solutions. He has authored *BizTalk 2013 EDI for Supply Chain Management, BizTalk 2010 EDI for Health Care, BizTalk 2006, 2010, and 2013 Recipes, Pro EDI in BizTalk Server 2006 R2, and Pro RFID in BizTalk Server 2009*. He has spoken at a number of venues, including Microsoft TechEd. In addition to Microsoft Dynamics CRM, he works with BizTalk, SharePoint, SQL Server, and custom .NET development. Mark, his wife Sara, and his boys Ciro and Iyer live somewhere in the rugged deserts and/or mountains of the American West. His web site is www.inotekgroup.com, and he can be contacted directly at mbeckner@inotekgroup.com.

**Triston Arisawa** brings a broad range of talents to any engagement, ranging from computer sciences to the culinary arts. He has extensive experience in the health care industry, working primarily with Microsoft BizTalk for HIPPA-compliant EDI solutions, utilizing many of the common EDI formats found in health care technology today. Specifically, he has managed several EDI projects involving small teams for EDI 834, 835, and 837 transactions. He has developed a number of Dynamics CRM solutions. Whether it's plugins or custom JavaScript for CRM 4.0, CRM 2011, 2013 on-premise or online—no project is too big or too small. Triston translates his desire for quality BizTalk and CRM implementations directly into success for his clients. He also makes one mean dragon roll (he has worked as a sushi chef in a variety of ritzy locations, including Aspen, Colorado). Triston holds several degrees, including a BS in Computer Information Systems, a BAS in Business Management, an AAS in Computer Aided Design, and an AAS in Culinary Arts. He can be reached at tarisawa@inotekgroup.com

# Plugins and Workflow Activities

## Chapter 1

Plugins and workflow activities are compiled as assemblies and run in the Global Assembly Cache (GAC). Some of the most complex CRM development is found in the .NET code associated with these two types of components. With CRM 2011, JScript and REST services provide a great deal of additional functionality that was not readily available in previous versions, such as creating and updating data. However, for many process and business requirements, plugin and workflow activity assemblies are still required.

This chapter outlines how to develop, register, and debug both types of components and introduces key concepts to working with data available through the CRM SDK.

## Developing Plugins

To demonstrate the development of a plugin, this chapter looks at a specific business case—the deactivation of the parent account of an opportunity, triggered when the opportunity has been lost. This allows for discussion of the overall structure of a plugin, illustrated by retrieving a related entity from within a plugin, setting the state on an entity, and sending an e-mail.

## Basic Code Framework for Plugins

All plugins begin with the same basic framework of code, which performs some context checking to ensure that the code fires only when expected. The basic code framework is shown in Listing 1-1, along with the additional context checks that ensure that it's triggering only on the loss of an opportunity.

*Listing 1-1.* Basic Plugin Framework, Executing on Loss of an Opportunity

```
using System;
using System.Collections.Generic;
using System.Linq;
using System.Text;
using Microsoft.Xrm.Sdk;
```

```csharp
using Microsoft.Xrm.Sdk.Query;
using Microsoft.Xrm.Sdk.Messages;
using System.Runtime.Serialization;
using Microsoft.Crm.Sdk.Messages;

namespace DemoPlugin
{
 public class Opportunity:IPlugin
 {
  public void Execute(IServiceProvider serviceProvider)
  {
   IPluginExecutionContext context =
   (IPluginExecutionContext)serviceProvider
.GetService(typeof(IPluginExecutionContext));
   if (context == null)
   {
    throw new ArgumentNullException("localContext");
   }
   IOrganizationServiceFactory serviceFactory =
(IOrganizationServiceFactory)serviceProvider
.GetService(typeof(IOrganizationServiceFactory));

   IOrganizationService service = serviceFactory
.CreateOrganizationService(context.InitiatingUserId);

   // specific code for a specific business case, you
will want to modify at this point for your own
   // business needs
   if (context.InputParameters.Contains("OpportunityClose")
    && context.InputParameters["OpportunityClose"] is Entity)
   {
    Entity EntityOpportunityClose = (Entity)context.Input
Parameters["OpportunityClose"];
    if (EntityOpportunityClose.LogicalName != "opportunityclose")
    {
     return;
    }
    if (context.MessageName == "Lose")
    {
     // core functionality goes here
    }
   }
  }
 }
}
```

## Core Functionality for Plugins

Once you have the basic framework in place, you can move on to the core functionality. This plugin fires on the loss of an opportunity, which means only a small number of all of the opportunity properties are available by default. The first thing to do is query the opportunity record for additional properties that will be used in the logic of this plugin.

## Querying Data

Querying an entity is very common functionality. You should break out querying into a separate function that can be called from a variety of locations. You may decide that you want to break all your common "utility" functions out into a separate class or assembly that can be referenced by any of your projects. Listing 1-2 shows the code for a generic method that can be used to query an entity by its GUID and return all its attributes.

*Listing 1-2.* GetEntity Method Returns All Attributes of a Specific Record

```
private Entity GetEntity(Guid
entityid,IOrganizationService service,String entity)
{
 Entity resultEntity = null;
 RetrieveMultipleRequest getRequest = new
RetrieveMultipleRequest();
 QueryExpression qex = new QueryExpression(entity);
 qex.ColumnSet = new ColumnSet() { AllColumns = true };
 qex.Criteria.FilterOperator = LogicalOperator.And;
 qex.Criteria.AddCondition(new ConditionExpression(entity
+ "id", ConditionOperator.Equal, entityid));
 getRequest.Query = qex;
 RetrieveMultipleResponse returnValues =
(RetrieveMultipleResponse)service.Execute(getRequest);
 resultEntity = returnValues.EntityCollection
.Entities[0];
 return resultEntity;
}
```

There are many ways to perform queries. In this case, the `retrieveMultiple` method is used, which will return an `EntityCollection` (array of zero to many entity records). Because the GUID is used to do the lookup, it is guaranteed that only a single record will ever be returned, so the first value in the array (`Entities[0]`) is forcibly returned.

## Setting State

The next step in this plugin's flow of logic is to set the state of the associated parent account record to `InActive`. For most properties on an entity, you can set the value through a single line of code (for example, setting the value of a string property is a simple assignment line of code). But for setting state, things are substantially more involved. In this case, you want to write another method that will let you set the state on a variety of entities so that the code can be contained and reused.

Listing 1-3 shows a method that sets the state of an entity by passing in the entity name and the GUID. In this case, the entity will always be set to `InActive`, but additional parameters to this method could be added to make it dynamic, too.

*Listing 1-3.* Setting the State and Status of an Entity

```
private void SetEntityStatus(IOrganizationService
service, Guid recordGUID, string entityName)
{
 SetStateRequest setState = new SetStateRequest();
 setState.EntityMoniker = new EntityReference();
 setState.EntityMoniker.Id = recordGUID;
 setState.EntityMoniker.Name = entityName;
 setState.EntityMoniker.LogicalName = entityName;

 //Setting 'State' (0 - Active ; 1 - InActive)
 setState.State = new OptionSetValue();
 setState.State.Value =  1;

 //Setting 'Status' (1 - Active ; 2 - InActive)
 setState.Status = new OptionSetValue();
 setState.Status.Value =  2;
 SetStateResponse setStateResponse =
(SetStateResponse)service.Execute(setState);
}
```

## Sending E-mail

CRM can send e-mail. This is done, as shown in Listing 1-4, with the following actions:

1.  The opportunity record is passed in, along with the service information and the opportunity ID.

2.  A message body is assigned (this can be dynamic and can include HTML for formatting). The message body will be the body of the e-mail.

3. The To and From e-mail addresses are assigned by setting the entity GUID for the system user and assigning them to an `ActivityParty` object.

4. The regarding object is set to the opportunity (this allows the e-mail to be linked to the opportunity record in CRM for tracking purposes).

5. Finally, the e-mail properties are set, and the e-mail is created and sent.

*Listing 1-4.* Creating an E-mail

```
public void CreateEmail(Entity opportunity,
IOrganizationService service,Guid oppId)
{
 string msg = "Dear Owner: <br/><br/> Please review the
opportunity.";
 string recipient = opportunity.Attributes["new_
manager"].ToString();

 ActivityParty fromParty = new ActivityParty
 {
  PartyId = new EntityReference("systemuser",new
Guid("620FA4D5-1656-4DDF-946F-20E6B1F19447"))
 };

 ActivityParty toParty = new ActivityParty
 {
  PartyId = new EntityReference("systemuser",  new
Guid(recipient))
 };

 EntityReference regarding = new
EntityReference("opportunity", oppId);

 Email email = new Email
 {
  To = new ActivityParty[] { toParty },
  From = new ActivityParty[] { fromParty },
  Subject = opportunity.Attributes["new_
titleanddescription"].ToString(),
  Description = msg,
  RegardingObjectId = regarding
 };

 service.Create(email);
}
```

## Tying It Together

With all the methods defined, and the core plugin framework code in place, you simply have to tie it together with the code shown in Listing 1-5. This code replaces the `// core functionality goes here` comment in Listing 1-1.

*Listing 1-5.* Core Functionality of the Plugin: Tying It Together

```
if (context.MessageName == "Lose")
{
 Entity Opportunity = null;
 Opportunity = GetEntity(((Microsoft.Xrm.Sdk
.EntityReference)
  (EntityOpportunityClose.Attributes["opportunityid"]))
.Id, service,"opportunity");

 // if the opportunity record has a parent account
associated with it, continue the logic execution
 if(Opportunity.Contains("parentaccountid"))
 {
  parentAccount = GetEntity(((Microsoft.Xrm.Sdk
.EntityReference)
    (Opportunity.Attributes["parentaccountid"])).Id,
service, "account");

  SetEntityStatus(service, ((Microsoft.Xrm.Sdk
.EntityReference)
    (Opportunity.Attributes["parentaccountid"])).Id,
"account");

  CreateEmail(opportunity, service,
EntityOpportunityClose.Attributes["opportunityid"])).Id);
 }
}
```

## Developing Workflow Activities

Workflow activity development is very similar to plugin development. Differences include the class (which inherits from **CodeActivity**) and the way the context, service, and service factory are created. The code in Listing 1-6 shows the framework for a workflow. The comment **// core functionality goes here** is where the custom code for each workflow activity you are creating begins.

*Listing 1-6.* Workflow Activity

```
using System;
using System.Collections.Generic;
using System.Linq;
using System.Text;
using System.Activities;
using Microsoft.Xrm.Sdk;
using Microsoft.Xrm.Sdk.Workflow;
using Microsoft.Xrm.Sdk.Query;
using Microsoft.Xrm.Sdk.Messages;
using Microsoft.Xrm.Sdk.Client;
using Microsoft.Xrm.Sdk.Discovery;
using System.Runtime.Serialization;
using Microsoft.Crm.Sdk.Messages;

namespace LeaseWorkflowActivity
{
 public class LeaseRecurringWorkflow: CodeActivity
 {
  protected override void Execute(CodeActivityContext
executionContext)
  {
   IWorkflowContext context = executionContext
.GetExtension<IWorkflowContext>();
   IOrganizationServiceFactory serviceFactory =
executionContext.GetExtension<IOrganizationServiceFactory>();

   IOrganizationService service = serviceFactory
.CreateOrganizationService(context.UserId);

   // core functionality goes here
  }
 }
}
```

> ■ **Note** CRM Online doesn't provide a way to schedule workflows. If you want to set up a recurring workflow (which is a common way to call workflow activities repeatedly), you need to configure your workflow as both an *on demand* and a *child* workflow (see Figure 1-1). You then need to set the wait state and duration, as shown in Figure 1-2. To initiate the workflow, you need to kick it off manually (on demand). Once started, it will continue to call itself as indicated in the schedule. Remember: CRM has a built-in process that ensures infinite loops are terminated. This means for recurring workflows, you can't schedule the workflow to occur more frequently than seven times in an hour—anything more will cause the workflow to terminate.

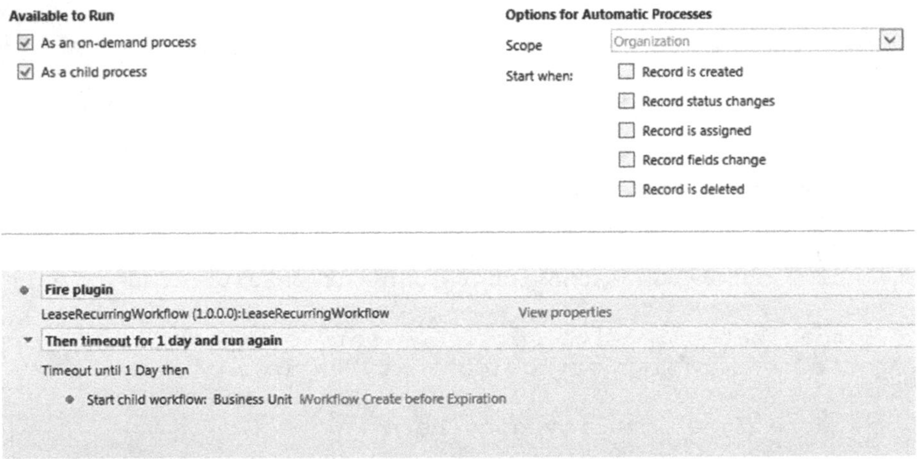

Figure 1-1. Allowing for a recurring workflow in CRM Online

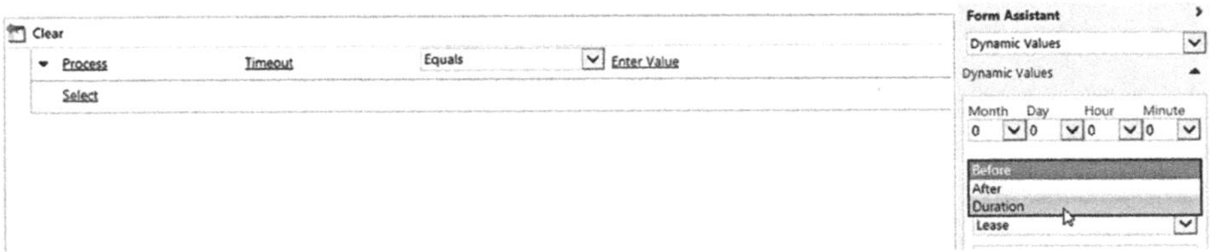

Figure 1-2. The Workflow Scheduler

# Plugin and Workflow Activity Registration

The Plugin Registration tool is critical component of plugins and workflow activity registration—yet it seems almost an afterthought. Over the years, the tool has gone through several updates, but it exists as a separate application from CRM and has a true "developer" feel about it. Though it looks and feels like something that isn't quite production ready, the tool's functionality and purpose are absolutely vital to the success of deploying and configuring your components.

## *Setting Up the Plugin Registration Tool*

The registration tool (pluginregistration.exe) is located in the SDK\bin folder of the CRM SDK, which you can download from `www.microsoft.com/en-us/download/details.aspx?id=24004`. Once you run this application, you're asked to set several properties. Take the following steps to set up your connection:

1. Click Create New Connection.

2. In the Label property, give the connection an appropriate name (such as the name of the environment you are connecting to).

3. In the Discovery URL property, set the value to what is specific to your environmental settings. To get this value, click Developer Resources in the Customization settings of your CRM instance and look at Service Endpoints. You will find the URL value under Discovery Service, as shown in Figure 1-3. Enter the value of what you find before the /XRMServices folder (for example, in Figure 1-3, the value would be `https://disco.crm.dynamics.com`).

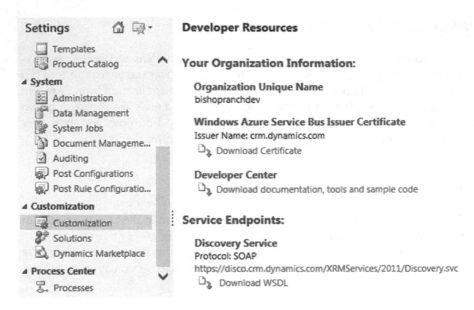

**Figure 1-3.** Discovery Service URL in Developer Resources

4. Enter your credentials in the User Name field (you will be prompted for a password after you click the Connect button).

Once you have successfully connected to your environment, a new connection will appear under Connections in your Plugin Registration tool. When you have connected to this new connection, you will see all the registered plugins and custom workflow activities listed in the window on the right, as shown in Figure 1-4.

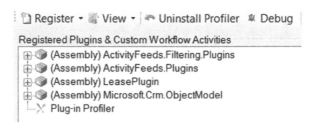

**Figure 1-4.** Viewing registered components

## Registering an Assembly

To register a plugin or workflow activity, click the Register option on the toolbar and select Register New Assembly (shown in Figure 1-5). The Register New Plugin screen that pops up is used for plugin and for workflow activity registration. Browse to your DLL (which may contain one or more plugins and activities) and click Load Assembly. Doing so lets you select which components to register and where to register them to.

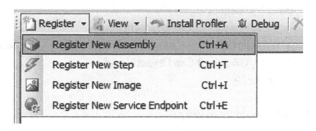

**Figure 1-5.** Register New Assembly

Next, set the Isolation Mode property to Sandbox. (In CRM Online, this value is always set to Sandbox, but in CRM on-premise you can chose between Sandbox and None, which allows for some level of control over trust level execution.) Set the Location where the Assembly should be stored to Database. Take note that when deploying to the database, you must also copy the DLL and PDB files to the \Server\ bin\assembly folder of your CRM installation to be able to debug. (This is noted in the Database setting area, shown in Figure 1-6.)

Step #3: Specify the Isolation Mode

◉ **Sandbox**
All code in this assembly will be run in a secure sandbox (reduced functionality)

◉ **None**

Step #4: Specify the Location where the Assembly should be stored

◉ **Database**
Assembly is stored and loaded from the database. For debugging purporses, the Symbols (.PDB files) must be in \Server\bin\assembly of the main installation folder for each server that needs to be debugged.

◉ **Disk**
Assembly is stored and loaded from \Server\bin\assembly in the main installation directory for each server. For debugging purposes, the Symbols (.PDB files) must be located in the same place as the assembly.

File Name on Server

◉ **GAC**
File is placed in the GAC of each server where it will used.

**Figure 1-6.** Sandbox and Database settings when registering plugin

> **Note**  When a workflow activity has been registered, it's marked with (Workflow Activity). Nothing further needs to be done once the assembly has been loaded (no steps need to be associated with it). See Figure 1-7.

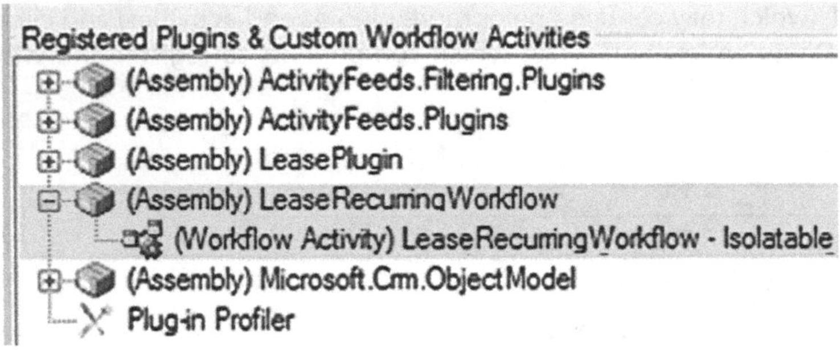

Figure 1-7. A registered workflow activity

## Registering a Step

Now that the assembly has been registered, next you must configure the settings for when it will execute by setting up one or more steps. For this example, take the opportunity plugin outlined earlier in this chapter. The business case for this plugin is that when an opportunity is lost, the associated account record will be deactivated. For the registration configuration, that means you have to set up a new step that triggers on the loss of an opportunity. Figure 1-8 shows how to configure the step for this scenario.

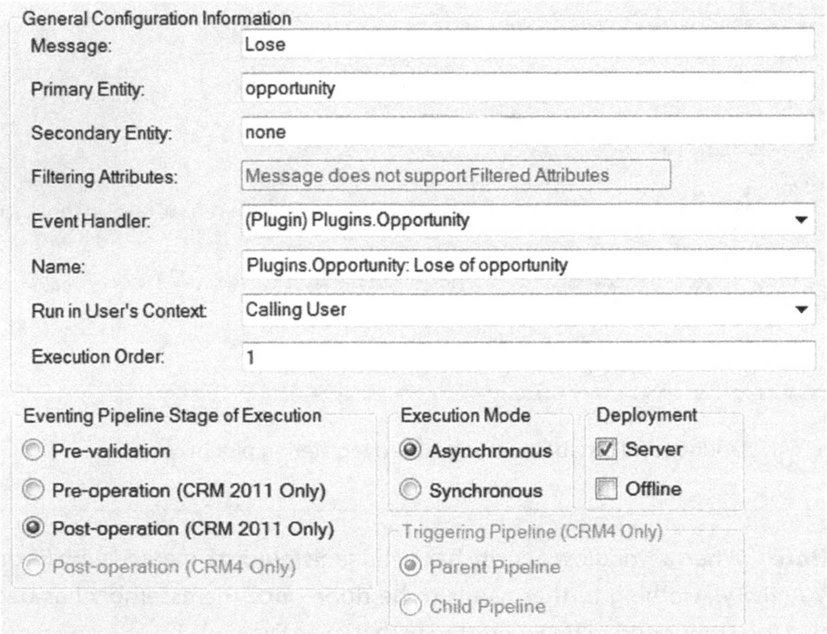

Figure 1-8. Configuring a step

Here are some of the key properties that are set here:

1. *Message:* This is the *event* occurring that will trigger the plugin to fire. There are dozens of potential events—or messages—that can be subscribed to. Press a single letter, and all the available messages starting with that letter are shown. In this case, when you press L, you see that Lose is one of three options.

2. *Primary Entity:* This is the name of the CRM entity that you will be registering the step to fire in conjunction with. All of the standard and custom entities within your environment will be listed here. In this case, type *opportunity*.

3. *Event Handler and Name:* These should default, but make sure they're set to appropriate values for your step.

4. *Run in User's Context:* This property is important. It determines the permissions that the plugin will fire under. If you want a plugin to execute exactly the same, regardless of which user is performing an action, set this to an account that has administrative privileges (such as CRM Admin). If you want this to be restricted to security settings that the user has defined, set it to Calling User.

5. *Eventing Pipeline Stage of Execution:* This setting will depend on what message you're setting the step to trigger on and when you want your plugin to fire. The loss of an opportunity should fire after the entity has been updated, so set this to Post-operation. Alternatively, you may want to set up a step that triggers on the creation of a new opportunity, and you need the plugin to fire before the opportunity is created. In that case, you would select Pre-validation.

6. *Execution Mode:* You can set this to Synchronous or Asynchronous. If you need to ensure that the plugin executes in full before the user can do anything else in CRM, set it to Synchronous.

---

**Note**   Registering a workflow activity doesn't require the additional step of registering a step. A workflow activity will execute from a step within a defined process in the CRM user interface, as shown in Figure 1-9. To access this, create a new workflow (process) from the Process menu option in Settings in the CRM user interface.

---

Figure 1-9. Workflow activity will be available in the Add Step window

# Debugging Plugins

After a plugin has been registered properly in a development setting, generally you want to work through debugging. Debugging a CRM on-premise solution is similar to debugging any ASP.NET application. And it requires fewer steps than debugging CRM Online. Debugging Online can be more time-consuming and therefore requires more thought and care in development. The following sections outline how to debug in both environments.

### Debugging CRM On-premise Solutions

When debugging on-premise, you can use Visual Studio to attach to a process and step through the code. The following steps are all that's required:

1. Make sure that the DLL and PDB that are built with your Visual Studio solution are current, and that the current builds of both are in the server/bin folder of your on-premise CRM installation folder. You need to register the plugins using the Plugin Registration tool prior to taking any further steps.

2. Click the Debug menu option in Visual Studio and select Attach to Process (see Figure 1-10). You want to attach to all instances of w3wp.exe listed in the Available Processes panel.

> **Note** When debugging workflow activities, you need to attach to the CrmAsyncService process in the Available Processes panel (w3wp.exe is the process to attach to for plugin debugging).

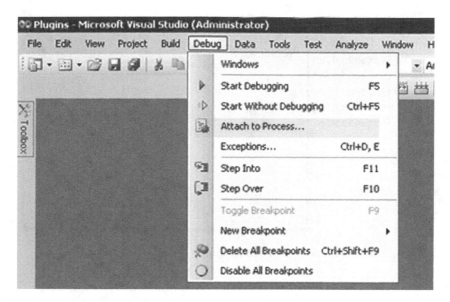

Figure 1-10. Attach to Process

> ■ **Note** When debugging on a remote server, you need to use the Visual Studio Remote Debugger and configure Visual Studio to connect to the target machine.

## Debugging CRM Online Plugins

CRM Online can't be debugged in the same way as CRM on-premise because there is no way to attach the Visual Studio environment directly to CRM Online. Instead, you need to take several steps to allow for debugging. This section describes those steps.

### Installing the Profiler

The first step to debugging in the CRM Online environment is to install the profiler. You do that by opening the Plugin Registration tool and connecting to the instance that has the plugin you want to debug. Click the Install Profiler button on the menu bar (see Figure 1-11).

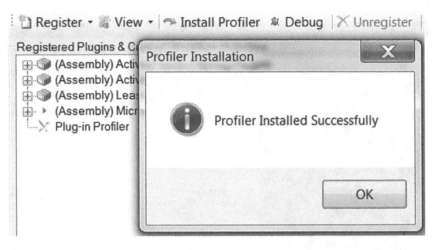

Figure 1-11. Installing the profiler for debugging

> ■ **Note** To uninstall the profiler, make sure you click the Uninstall Profiler but-ton in the Plugin Registration tool. If you simply unregister it (as you would any-thing else registered), you'll leave a lot of pieces installed and will have some additional cleanup work to do.

## Profiling a Step

With the profiler installed, the next step is to right-click the step within a plugin that you want to debug and select the Start Profiling option. In the Profiler Settings (shown in Figure 1-12), you can set various properties. You can generally use the default settings here and simply click OK. Once a step has been configured with the profiler, it will have a note next to it in the Plugin Registration tool that says (Profiled) (see Figure 1-13). You can add profiling to as many steps as you need to successfully debug your code.

Step #1: Specify Profile Storage

◉ **Exception (Recommended)**

When the profiled component is triggered, an exception will be thrown with the compressed profile in the error message.

○ **Persist to Entity**

The profile will be stored in a custom entity for each profiled operation that occurs.

Persistence Key: 725cd346c07449c98f2317e1c88dcf64

Step #2: Set Profiler Settings

☐ **Limit Number of Executions**

Maximum # of Executions: 1

☑ **Include Secure Configuration**

Includes the secure configuration value in the profile for more comprehensive debugging. Please note that the Secure Configuration may include sensitive data.

| OK | Cancel |

Figure 1-12. Profiler Settings on Step

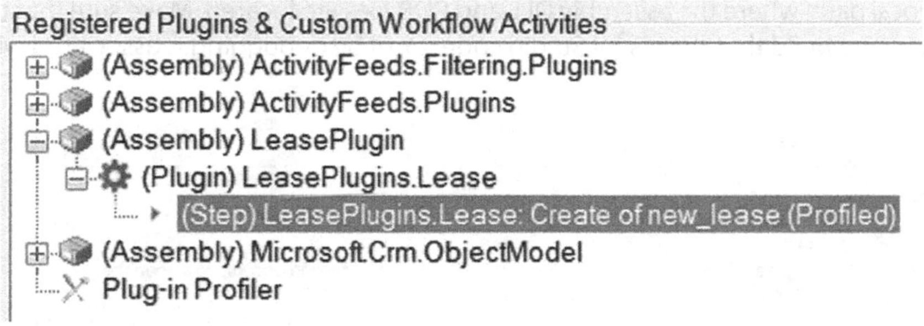

Registered Plugins & Custom Workflow Activities

⊞ (Assembly) ActivityFeeds.Filtering.Plugins
⊞ (Assembly) ActivityFeeds.Plugins
⊟ (Assembly) LeasePlugin
  ⊟ (Plugin) LeasePlugins.Lease
    ▸ (Step) LeasePlugins.Lease: Create of new_lease (Profiled)
⊞ (Assembly) Microsoft.Crm.ObjectModel
  ✕ Plug-in Profiler

Figure 1-13. A step with profiler attached (Profiled)

## Triggering the Profiler and Saving the Log File

Now that the step is successfully profiled, you need to trigger the code behind the step to execute. Go into the CRM Online front end and force the action to occur that will trigger the step (for example, if the step is on the loss of an opportunity, go into an opportunity and click Lost Opportunity). When the code is hit, an error similar to that shown In Figure 1-14 will pop up. Click the Download Log File button and save it.

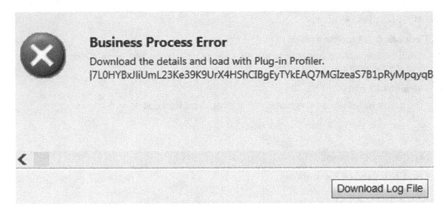

**Figure 1-14.** Error indicating that the profiler was successfully triggered

## Debugging, Attaching, and Breakpoints

Back in the Plugin Registration tool, click the Debug button (on the menu, next to the Uninstall Profiler button). The Debug Existing Plug-in dialogue box shown in Figure 1-15 opens. Set the Profile Location property to the local path where you downloaded the log file (Figure 1-14). The Assembly Location property should be the local path where the assembly DLL and PDB files are located. Make sure that this is the same build that the Visual Studio code you'll be debugging is associated with.

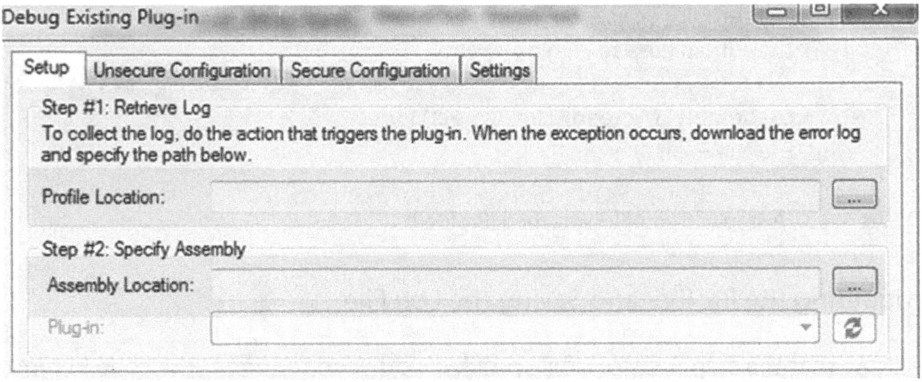

**Figure 1-15.** Debug Existing Plug-in dialog box

Open your plugin code in Visual Studio and set breakpoints where appropriate. You should start by putting a breakpoint on the first piece of code that will execute when triggered, so that you can ensure all your code is firing as expected.

Once your breakpoints are set, click the Debug option on the menu bar in Visual Studio and select Attach to Process. In the Available Processes panel, highlight the pluginregistration.exe process and click the Attach button.

Finally, once everything is attached in Visual Studio, click the Start Execution button in the Debug Existing Plug-in tool (Figure 1-16). You will now be able to step through your code.

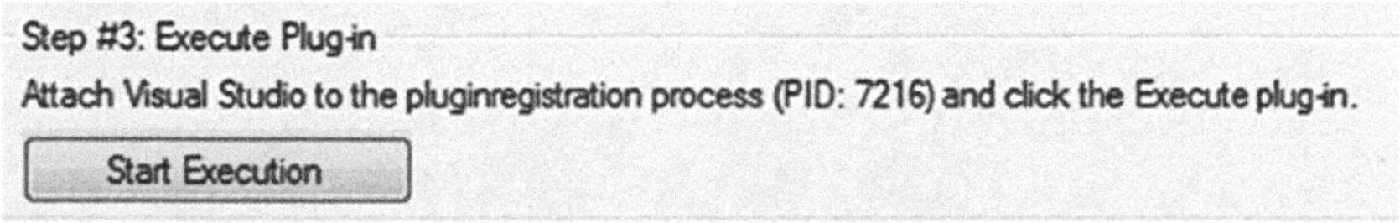

Step #3: Execute Plug-in

Attach Visual Studio to the pluginregistration process (PID: 7216) and click the Execute plug-in.

Start Execution

*Figure 1-16. Start Execution*

## Conclusion

You've looked at how to develop and register plugins and workflow activities and have worked through some of the critical aspects to querying and modifying data. You've also stepped through debugging plugins in on-premise and CRM Online environments. Plugins and workflow activities will be some of the most labor-intensive activities that you do in CRM. But they can be optimized and made maintainable through intelligent planning and coding. Developing these components introduces you to interacting with CRM through the SDK, which is essential to building external applications that can pull data from and write records to CRM. Those topics are covered in the next chapter.

# .NET Apps and the CRM SDK

Working with CRM from external .NET applications and assemblies is an important activity, and one which the CRM SDK readily supports. There are many examples of real-world cases where you may want to write code to communicate with CRM. Some of these cases involve integration and migration of data, which are covered in Chapter 3. Other cases are for small loads of data, pulls of data for reporting purposes, and views into data for external applications. This chapter outlines how to write a C# assembly that will read from and write to CRM. It also discusses how to write CRM data to SQL Server.

## Building an Application and Assembly

Using Visual Studio, create a solution that contains a C# Windows Forms Application and a C# class library assembly (see Figure 2-1). The form has a button on it that calls the assembly. The assembly contains all the business logic that will read data from and write data to CRM.

**Figure 2-1.** C# Windows Forms Application

Once the solution has been created with the two projects, you need to add references to several CRM assemblies. You can access those two assemblies in the CRM SDK in sdk\bin. A full list of all assemblies required in the class library, along with the structure of the two projects in the solution, is shown in Figure 2-2.

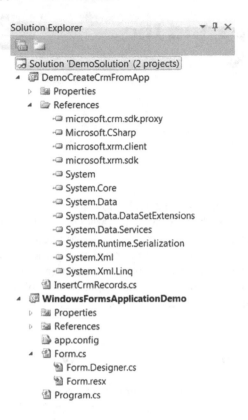

**Figure 2-2.** References and solution structure

## References

The Windows Form project needs to have a reference to the class library. The form is really just used to kick off the process for testing—a button can be dropped on it and tied to a method in the assembly. For this example, the process is going to retrieve account data from CRM and write that data to a local SQL table. Therefore, you can name the button InsertData and have code behind it similar to that shown in Listing 2-1. The code shows a reference being made to the class library and an instantiation of that class with the call to the `InsertToSql()` method.

*Listing 2-1.* Button Click on Form

```
using DemoCreateCrmFromApp;

private void button1_Click(object sender, EventArgs e)
{
  DemoCreateCrmFromApp.InsertCrmRecords obj = new
```

```
DemoCreateCrmFromApp.InsertCrmRecords();
 obj.InsertToSql();
}
```

## Calling the Assembly

With a click of the button, the call to the class library logic occurs. The value to containing this code in a class library is high. Here are some of the primary reasons for assemblies:

- Assemblies can be called from a variety of applications and platforms. This sample shows the assembly being called from a Windows Forms Application, but assemblies can be called from virtually any Microsoft technology or platform, including SQL Server, BizTalk, SharePoint, workflows, WCF and Web Services, and more.

- Code can be stored in the global assembly cache for ease of reference across a variety of applications.

- Assemblies can be versioned. This allows for multiple instances of the same assembly to exist in the Global Assembly Cache (GAC), with older versions of clients calling the assembly referencing older versions of the assembly. Newer clients can access new functionality.

## Retrieving CRM Data and Writing to SQL Server

The assembly for this example is made up of a class with several methods. The first is the `InsertToSql` method, the primary method callable from clients. It defines a connection string (which could be passed in as a parameter) and initiates a connection to CRM. Then it retrieves the accounts from CRM and inserts each of those accounts into a SQL table. The code for this main method is shown in Listing 2-2.

*Listing 2-2.* The Main Process

```
public void InsertToSql()
{
 string connectionString = "Url=https://myinstance.crm.
dynamics.com;
  Username=me@myinstance.onmicrosoft.com; Password=
p@ssword";
 Microsoft.Xrm.Client.CrmConnection connection =
CrmConnection.Parse(connectionString);
 var service = new OrganizationService(connection);
 var context = new CrmOrganizationServiceContext(connection);
```

```
EntityCollection accounts = getAccounts(service);
if (accounts.Entities.Count >= 1)
{
  for (int i = 0; i < accounts.Entities.Count; i++)
  {
   Entity account = accounts.Entities[i];
   insertSQL(account);
  }
 }
}
```

## Retrieving Data

There are two methods that deserve inspection here. The first is the getAccounts method (shown in full in Listing 2-3), which queries CRM and retrieves all the columns and all the accounts available. These are returned to the calling process in an EntityCollection and can be accessed like an array of objects in the loop in the main method.

*Listing 2-3.* Querying Accounts

```
public EntityCollection getAccounts(OrganizationService
service)
{
 RetrieveMultipleRequest getRequest = new
RetrieveMultipleRequest();
 QueryExpression qex = new QueryExpression("account");
 qex.ColumnSet = new ColumnSet() { AllColumns = true };

 getRequest.Query = qex;
 RetrieveMultipleResponse returnValues =
(RetrieveMultipleResponse)service.Execute(getRequest);
 return returnValues.EntityCollection;
}
```

## Writing to SQL Server

The second method to look at, shown in Listing 2-4, is the code that does the insertion of the data into SQL. This method uses a stored procedure to do the insertion and passes in several parameters based on the data that was returned in the account entity. The stored procedure, called insertSQL___, is shown in Listing 2-5.

*Listing 2-4.* Inserting CRM Data into SQL

```
public void insertSQL(Entity account)
{
 string sqlConnectionString = "Data
Source=server123;Initial Catalog=Demo;Integrated
Security=True";
 string storedProcedure = "spInsertAccount";

 SqlConnection sqlConnection = new SqlConnection
(sqlConnectionString);
 SqlCommand sqlCommand = new SqlCommand(storedProcedure,
sqlConnection);

 sqlCommand.CommandType = CommandType.StoredProcedure;
 sqlConnection.Open();

 SqlParameter paramAccountName = new SqlParameter();
 paramAccountName.Direction = ParameterDirection.Input;
 paramAccountName.ParameterName = "@AccountName";
 paramAccountName.Value = account.Attributes["name"];
 sqlCommand.Parameters.Add(paramAccountName);

 SqlParameter paramAccountId = new SqlParameter();
 paramAccountId.Direction = ParameterDirection.Input;
 paramAccountId.ParameterName = "@AccountId";
 paramAccountId.Value = account.Attributes["accountid"];
 sqlCommand.Parameters.Add(paramAccountId);

 SqlParameter paramAccountNumber = new SqlParameter();
 paramAccountNumber.Direction = ParameterDirection.Input;
 paramAccountNumber.ParameterName = "@AccountNumber";
 if(account.Attributes.Contains("accountnumber"))
 {
  paramAccountNumber.Value = account.
Attributes["accountnumber"];
 }
 else
 {
  paramAccountNumber.Value = "No Account Number";
 }
 sqlCommand.Parameters.Add(paramAccountNumber);

 sqlCommand.ExecuteNonQuery();
 sqlConnection.Close();
}
```

*Listing 2-5.* Stored Procedure Called for Inserting Records

```
CREATE PROCEDURE spInsertAccount
 -- Add the parameters for the stored procedure here
 @AccountName as nvarchar(100)
 ,@AccountId as nvarchar(40)
 ,@AccountNumber as nvarchar(20)
AS
BEGIN
 SET NOCOUNT ON;
 -- Insert statements for procedure here
 INSERT INTO [Demo].[dbo].[Account]
 ([AccountName]
  ,[AccountID]
  ,[AccountNumber]
  ,[InsertDate])
 VALUES
 (@AccountName
  ,@AccountId
  ,@AccountNumber
  ,GetDate())
END
```

The value of working through this exercise is to show what is required to pull data out of CRM and populate a table. When working with CRM Online, you will often find there are situations in which you need the data in a local environment—for example, when you need to write some local analytics for reporting. Chapter 3 introduces you to Scribe Online. One of its tools is Scribe Replication Services, which pulls data from CRM and writes it to a local database. You can see, based on the simple account scenario you just worked through, how this can be easily written for each entity you are interested in without needing to purchase a third-party tool. Recommendations for integrations are covered in Chapter 3, but from a purely code-centric perspective, working through each entity, pulling back all the fields, and storing the data locally are relatively easy.

# Creating and Deleting Records in CRM

Now that you've worked through the process of reading data from CRM and writing the foundational connectivity work, we give you a quick look at how to create and delete records. We use the same Visual Studio solution with the two projects.

## Creating a Record

For the creation of a record, instead of writing the set of accounts from CRM to SQL Server, we show how to write them to another entity instance in CRM. For ease of illustration, this entity is a duplicate of the account entity and is called `new_accountcopy`. Take the following steps to write this data to CRM:

1. Add another button to the form and tie the click event to a method in the C# class that contains the code to write to CRM. Listing 2-6 shows sample code that does this.

   *Listing 2-6.* Creating a New Record in CRM

   ```
   public void CreateNewAccount(Entity
   account,OrganizationService service)
   {
     Entity newAccount = new Entity("new_accountcopy");

     newAccount.Attributes["new_name"] = account.
   Attributes["name"];
     newAccount.Attributes["new_address1"] = account.
   Attributes["address1_line1"];
     newAccount.Attributes["new_city"] = account.
   Attributes["address1_city"];
     newAccount.Attributes["new_state"] = account.
   Attributes["address1_stateorprovince"];
     newAccount.Attributes["new_zipcode"] = account.
   Attributes["address1_postalcode"];
     service.Create(newAccount);
   }
   ```

2. In the loop from Listing 2-2, originally called the `insertSQL()` method, change this call to execute the method in Listing 2-6. The call can be performed as follows:

   ```
   CreateNewAccount(account,service);
   ```

## Deleting a Record

Deleting a record is simple, but it requires that you have the GUID of the record you want to delete. If you are creating the account, you can get the GUID and immediately delete the record, as shown in Listing 2-7. Obviously, in most cases you first need to do a query of the account records to get the GUID of the record you want to delete.

*Listing 2-7.* Create, Get GUID, Delete Record

```
// create the account record (an extension of what was in
Listing 2-6
Guid gd = service.Create(account);

//now Delete the account using the ID returned from the
create method
service.Delete("account", gd);
```

The demonstrations you've worked through have shown how to retrieve, create, and delete data, but you can also update, associate, and disassociate records (and perform several more actions). Become familiar with the Organization Service (called `service` in Listing 2-6), as it contains many of the most important methods for reading and writing data to and from CRM. It's not only used when interacting with the API through .NET, it's also used in JScript and REST calls (as discussed in Chapter 4).

## Using Early Bound Classes

Using the SDK is simple and lets you to accomplish whatever tasks are needed, but it also requires that you know the structure of your entities. For example, to set an attribute, you have to explicitly state the name of the attribute (`Attributes["new_name"]`, for example). There is no way in code to get access to all of the properties of your object, and you have to refer to the CRM entity via the customizations section in the user interface to find the names to the various fields. This is known as *late binding*, because the code you are writing does not have access to the object model at the time of development—only at runtime.

You can, however, take steps to work with CRM objects with early binding through the use of the CRM Service Utility. This utility can be used to generate a C# class you can add to your solution. Once added, you will have access to all of the fields and properties available on each entity through IntelliSense, and you won't have to know the names and types of objects in order to set, retrieve, and perform calculations on the various fields.

The CRM Service Utility, CrmSvcUtil.exe, can be found in the sdk\bin folder of the CRM SDK. A sample instance of the call from a command line is shown in Figure 2-3. The parameters you will most likely want to use are shown in Table 2-1 (you can see the full list by typing *CrmSvcUtil.exe /help* at the command line).

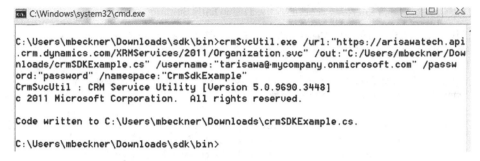

**Figure 2-3.** Executing the CRM Service Utility command line tool

**Table 2-1.** CRM Service Utility Parameters

| Query Option | Description |
|---|---|
| URL | This is the URL to the CRM Organization Service on-premise or Online instance. The full URL can be retrieved from the Developer Resources option on the Customization menu option of Settings (in the CRM web user interface). |
| out | Output directory where the C# file will be written that contains the definition for all entities and properties in your current CRM solution. |
| username | User name for the CRM environment you are connecting to. |
| password | Password for the CRM environment you are connecting to. |
| namespace | The namespace is how you will refer to all of the objects within the class that is being generated. You might want to get descriptive and name it something like CompanyName.CRM.Proxies. |

The file generated (shown in Figure 2-4) will contain all the entities and properties in your full CRM solution and can be fairly sizeable (in this case over 5 MB, and the CRM instance it was generated with had very few customizations).

| Name | Date modified | Type | Size |
|---|---|---|---|
| sdk | 8/26/2013 5:15 AM | File folder | |
| crmSDKExample.cs | 8/28/2013 5:18 AM | Visual C# Source fi... | 5,425 KB |

**Figure 2-4.** Generated file (note file size)

Add the file that was generated to the C# class library you developed earlier in this chapter. Once it is added, you can revise the code to create a record (shown earlier in Listing 2-6) to use early binding. All the entity properties are available to set in the code, as shown in Listing 2-8. Figure 2-5 demonstrates how properties are now available on the account entity in IntelliSense.

*Listing 2-8.* The CreateNewAccount Method using Early Binding

```
public void CreateNewAccountEarlyBound(CrmSdkExample.
Account account, OrganizationService service)
{
 CrmSdkExample.new_accountcopy newAccount = new
CrmSdkExample.new_accountcopy();

 newAccount.new_name = account.Name;
 newAccount.new_address1 = account.Address1_Line1;
 newAccount.new_City = account.Address1_City;
 newAccount.new_State = account.Address1_StateOrProvince;
 newAccount.new_ZipCode = account.Address1_PostalCode;

 service.Create(newAccount);
}
```

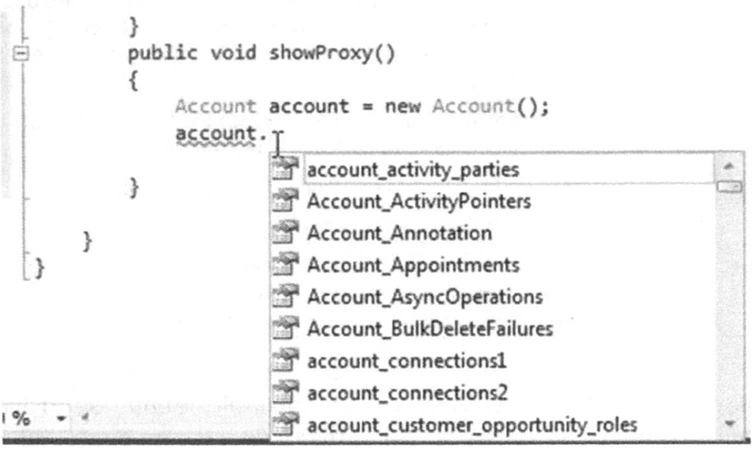

**Figure 2-5.** Properties available at design time with early binding

## Conclusion

By working through the various scenarios outlined in this chapter, you should be able to leverage the power of the SDK to implement whatever solution you need in .NET. You can use late bound or early bound classes, depending on your preference (which should be dictated by the complexity of your entities and their related fields). Inserting, updating, deleting, and retrieving data can all be done through the SDK with minimal effort.

Many requirements may lead you to developing your own custom .NET solutions to interact with the CRM SDK API, but integration and migration are the two most obvious. We cover those topics in Chapter 3.

# Integration and Migration | Chapter 3

Requirements for integration and migration of data to and from a CRM environment come in many flavors. The type of CRM environment (CRM 2011 Online versus on-premise and CRM 4.0), the systems being integrated with (other versions of CRM, databases such as Oracle and SQL, or back-end systems like finance), and the direction of the data (pulling from CRM or writing to CRM) are all factors that will influence your decision-making around appropriate technology and architecture. This chapter looks at several patterns and applications of technology, including custom code, database components, and Scribe Online. Although there are many factors, and integration can be challenging from an architectural aspect, creating a final solution that is easy to develop and maintain is possible.

## Custom-Coded Solutions

Chapter 2 goes into details about how to build out an external application to read from and write data to CRM. The chapter outlines how to call the CRM API and work with SQL Server. You should be able to extrapolate the primary ideas behind a custom-coded integration or migration from this overview. However, the following is not accounted for:

1. *Exception handling:* Generally an afterthought of development, exception handling becomes a topic of architectural concern in an integration/migration scenario. What happens when 10,000 records are being written and the 5,000th one fails? How can you resume processing from that point, and how do you notify and log the process? Many aspects of exception handling must be considered and coded for, and you should expect to set aside a large chunk of your development time to address these questions.

2. *Logging:* Where will you log your progress, how much detail will be kept, and how will that information be accessed? Is it only available to the developer running it, or can other users who need it view it?

3.  *Retries:* If data fails to insert, how will you retry it until it does work? When dealing with a handful of records, this isn't a big deal. But when working with tens or hundreds of thousands of records, you need to have a robust retry process in place.

4.  *Mapping:* Mapping data from one entity to another is a requirement for every integration and migration project. For every entity, you must think through how to keep your mapping clean, intelligible, and maintainable, because it is guaranteed to change throughout the development and load cycle. One entity alone (such as `account`) may have more than 100 fields that need to be mapped, and it can be overwhelming to code all this and maintain it so that it can be worked with and kept clean.

5.  *Lookups:* In virtually every entity mapping, lookups are necessary. You need to determine how that will be done— via configuration file, database table, lookups in CRM, and so on.

6.  *Performance:* When moving large amounts of data, how will you ensure that the application is optimized and can run successfully with the data loads required?

---

**Note**   In the custom code approach, not only do you have to work through the mapping of data, you also have to build out the code that pulls the data from the source system, writes it to the target system, handles exceptions, retries, and notifications, and so on. The volume of coding required in a custom integration can be staggering. When migrating or integrating data between two CRM environments, or between CRM and a SQL database, Oracle database, or SalesForce, you should almost always use Scribe Online. When migrating between other types of systems and environments, you should use custom code or integration platforms like Microsoft BizTalk Server.

---

You will have to work through many topics to build a custom integration or migration. Generally speaking, you should not be coding your own from scratch. Certainly there are scenarios in which you need to work through your own code. But in general you should look for tools that have already been developed and that handle these core pieces of functionality out of the box, so that you can focus primarily on the mapping requirements of your solution. One such tool is Scribe Online, covered in the next section.

# Scribe Online

Migration and integration using Scribe Online is a commonly recommended approach. Extremely intuitive and easy to use, the tool eliminates most of the grunt work associated with the movement of data. You can focus entirely on the mapping of data between systems and ignore all the core code that comes with a custom-coded solution. This section outlines how to build out a migration from CRM on-premise to CRM Online. Armed with the knowledge in this chapter, you will be able to develop a fully functional Scribe Online implementation.

## *Migrating Data from CRM 2011 on-premise to CRM Online*

Using Scribe Online to migrate data one time from CRM on-premise to CRM Online is fairly straightforward. The tasks required consist of installing an agent, setting up connections for both systems, and building out the maps for the entities that will be migrated. The interface is simple to understand. The main menu, along with a single solution for Integration Services, is shown in Figure 3-1.

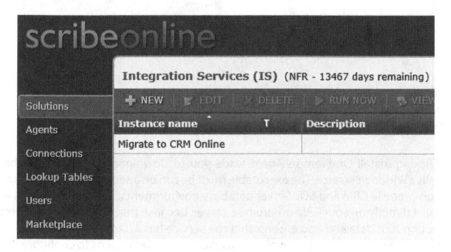

Figure 3-1. The Scribe Online menu

This section looks at creating an agent and configuration connections, working with maps in solutions, and building lookup tables.

## Configuring an Agent

The first step in setting up your Scribe Online environment is to create an agent. Currently two agent types are available, but you will need to use the On-Premise Agent because the source system in this scenario is on-premise. If both of environments were CRM Online, you could use the Cloud Agent option. In Scribe, from the Agents menu option, click the New button and click the Install On-Premise Agent button, as shown in Figure 3-2.

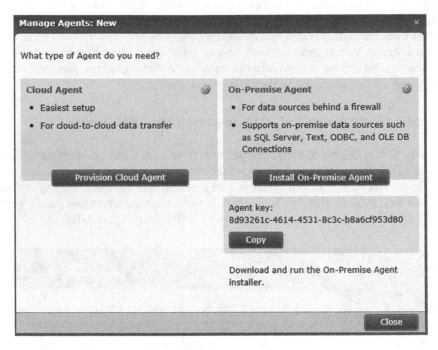

**Figure 3-2.** Downloading the On-Premise Agent

Clicking Install On-Premise Agent leads you to download an executable that installs a Windows service. The executable must be run on a server that has access to the on-premise CRM and SQL Server database environments. The ideal option is to install it directly on your CRM on-premise server, because that provides for the best throughput of data and also ensures that the service has access to everything.

Once the executable has downloaded, take the following steps to configure it:

1. On the System Configuration Check page, address any errors that may be indicated and click Next.

2. Click Next in the Welcome screen.

3. In the Agent Key property on the Enter Agent Key page, enter the GUID value that was shown when you downloaded the executable (see "Agent key" in Figure 3-2).

4. Set an appropriate destination folder on the Destination Folder screen and complete the Wizard to complete installation of the solution.

## Configuring Connections

When the installation package has completed, you will see a new service agent displayed in the Agents menu of Scribe Online. This agent enables communication between Scribe Online and the environment where the agent was installed. But first you must set up a new connection to give the right credentials and connectivity information.

To configure a new connection, take the following steps:

1. From the Connections menu option, click New to open the configuration screen for a new connection.

2. For the Type property, select the appropriate connector option (see Figure 3-3). In the case of migrating from CRM on-premise, you have two options: Microsoft Dynamics CRM and Microsoft SQL Server. In most scenarios, you should use the Microsoft Dynamics CRM option. But you will find that, because the two entity structures are nearly identical between CRM 2011 on-premise and CRM Online, you can use either of these for most of the data you will be migrating. Later in this section, you will look at migrating data with both of them.

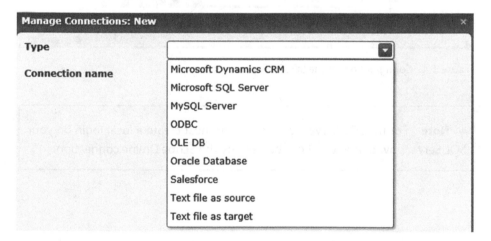

**Figure 3-3.** Connection Type options

3. Depending on which Type of connector you select, you can configure a variety of different parameters . Figures 3-4 and 3-5 show the settings available for the Microsoft SQL Server and the Microsoft Dynamics CRM connectors. You can pattern your own configured settings from what you see illustrated in these figures.

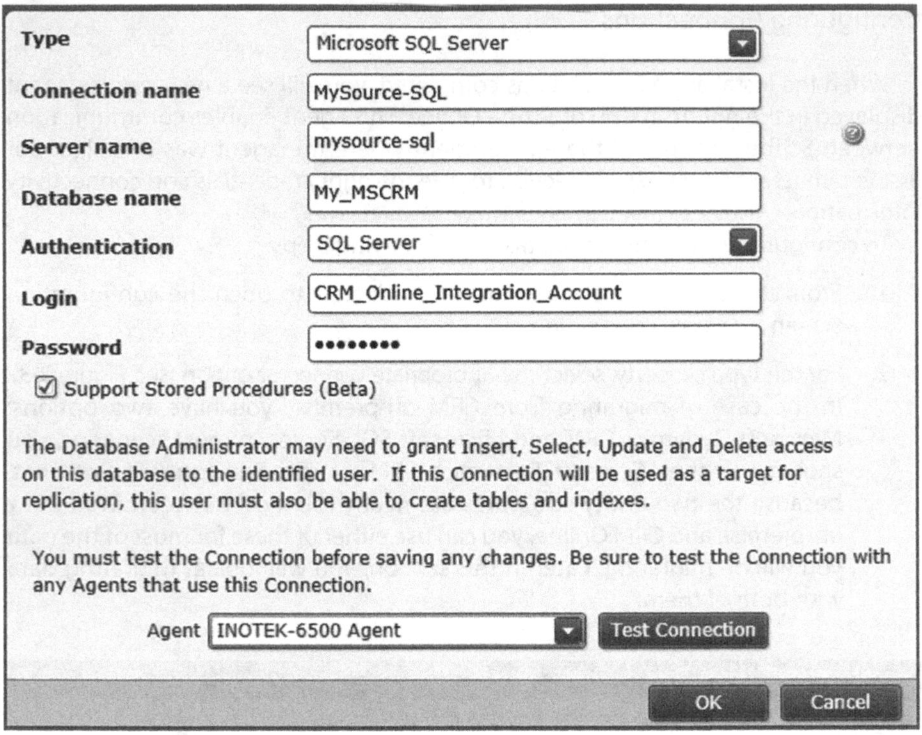

| Type | Microsoft SQL Server |
| --- | --- |
| Connection name | MySource-SQL |
| Server name | mysource-sql |
| Database name | My_MSCRM |
| Authentication | SQL Server |
| Login | CRM_Online_Integration_Account |
| Password | •••••••• |

☑ Support Stored Procedures (Beta)

The Database Administrator may need to grant Insert, Select, Update and Delete access on this database to the identified user. If this Connection will be used as a target for replication, this user must also be able to create tables and indexes.

You must test the Connection before saving any changes. Be sure to test the Connection with any Agents that use this Connection.

Agent | INOTEK-6500 Agent |    Test Connection

OK    Cancel

Figure 3-4. Configuration for the SQL Server connector

■ **Note**   For the SQL Server connector, you must create a local login on your SQL Server environment that can be used by the Scribe Online connection.

| | |
|---|---|
| Type | Microsoft Dynamics CRM ▼ |
| Connection name | MySource On Premise |
| Deployment | On-Premise ▼ |
| CRM URL | http://mysourcecrm:5555 |
| User ID | mysource_domain\crmadmin |
| | ex: domain\UserId |
| Password | •••••• |
| Organization | MySourceOrg  [Browse] |
| | CRM Organization is case-sensitive |

☑ Include picklist display names

The Dynamics CRM user must have read and bulk delete privileges as well as appropriate permissions to create entities and register plug-ins.

You must test the Connection before saving any changes. Be sure to test the Connection with any Agents that use this Connection.

Agent [INOTEK-6500 Agent ▼]  [Test Connection]

[OK]  [Cancel]

Figure 3-5. Configuration for the Dynamics CRM connector (On-Premise deployment)

> ■ **Note** For the Dynamics CRM connector used in an on-premise connection, the CRM URL should be the base URL you use to open your on-premise CRM instance in a browser. You must include the full URL, including the port (defaulted to 5555 in Figure 3-5). Once you have the URL and credentials configured, you will be able to click the Browse button to get the proper organization name for the Organization property.

For the purposes of this chapter, a total of three connections will be used. One connection is for the source connectivity to the CRM on-premise instance using the Microsoft Dynamics CRM connector. The second is for the source connectivity to the CRM SQL Server using the Microsoft SQL Server connector. The final connection is for the target CRM Online environment (the properties for this are shown in Figure 3-6).

| Type | Microsoft Dynamics CRM | ▼ |
| --- | --- | --- |
| Connection name | CRM Online Development | |
| Deployment | Online | ▼ |
| CRM Online URL | https://disco.crm.dynamics.com | |
| | ex: https://disco.crm.dynamics.com | |
| Windows Live ID | c-markb@mydevinstance.onmicrosoft.com | |
| Password | •••••••• | |
| Organization | MyTargetOrg | Browse |
| | CRM Organization is case-sensitive | |

Figure 3-6. Configuration for the Dynamics CRM connector (Online deployment)

## Configuring an Integration Services Solution

Now that your connections have been fully configured, you can create a new Integration Services solution. In the Integration Services window of Scribe Online, click New to create a new instance, and take the following steps:

1. On the General tab, give the solution an appropriate name and description. The solution can be enabled or disabled as a whole by clicking the Enabled property on this screen.

2. On the Agent tab, select the agent you configured earlier in this chapter.

3. Skip the Maps tab for now (you will create two maps in the next section).

4. On the Schedule tab, you can set up the solution to run on whatever schedule you want. Because most migrations run only once, you most likely want to set this to On Demand. Certainly, during development you will want it left on this default setting so you can control when the solution runs. To start the solution when it is set to On Demand, simply right-click it on the main screen and select Run Now, as shown in Figure 3-7.

**Figure 3-7.** Right-click a solution to start it manually

## Creating Maps

The previous steps should take you about 20 minutes to work through, which means the only real time with Scribe Online is invested in developing and testing your maps. This section looks at two maps: one is for the mapping of e-mail activities and the other is for the mapping of annotations (which includes file attachments). For the source, the e-mail activity mapping will use the SQL Server connection you configured (Figure 3-4), and the annotation/attachment mapping will use the Dynamics on-premise connection )) (Figure 3-5). For the target, both will use the Dynamics Online connection (Figure 3-6).

> **Note** You can create Basic and Advanced maps with Scribe Online. You can migrate 100% of your data using Basic maps, as long as you ensure that the execution order is correct. For example, if you are migrating activities, you must ensure that the Regarding Objects (set in fields such as regardingobjectid) are mapped first. This means that if you have task activities associated with leads and accounts, the leads and accounts must be migrated before the tasks (so that the IDs exist in the target system). With Advanced maps, you can set them up to migrate all the associated data at once. In some cases, you may have entities that are interrelated (such as contacts that are associated with accounts and vice-versa). In these cases, you will have to run the migration on these objects several times. The first time, migrate them without the mapping of their related fields. Once loaded, run the integration again, this time with the related fields mapped.
>
> A word of caution: you will spend far more time working with the Advanced maps than with the Basic maps, even if you have many interrelated entities that must be mapped in a certain order.

To create a map, you need to set properties on two tabs: the Connections tab and the Fields tab. The Connections tab should have the source connectivity information required for the source data. The Connection property and the Entity property are set to the appropriate values for what you are mapping. For purposes of this chapter, the Email properties should be set to those shown in Figure 3-8, while the Annotation properties should be configured like those in Figure 3-9.

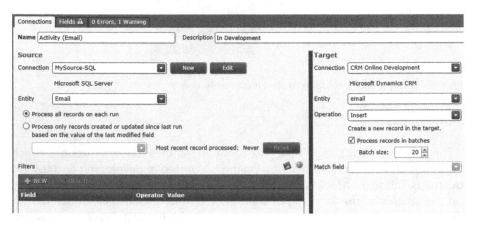

**Figure 3-8.** The Connections tab for e-mail activity migration

---

■ **Note**   When migrating entities with thousands of records, it is good to set the Batch Size property to a small number, at least during test and development. This property defaults to 2000, but setting it lower allows you to manually stop the process much more quickly if you see large numbers of errors being thrown when you start the process.

---

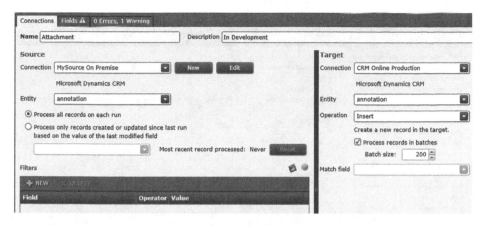

**Figure 3-9.** The Connections tab for annotation/attachment migration

> ▨ **Note** There are two types of attachments: those associated with notes/an-notations and those associated with e-mails. Scribe Online supports the migra-tion of attachments associated only with annotations. If you want to migrate e-mail attachments, you need to write custom code to do it. Also note that the maximum value for the Batch Size property that can be set when migrating attachments with annotations is 200 (anything more will throw an error).

## Mapping Email Activities and Using Lookup Tables

With the Connection tab configured, you can now focus on the field mapping. Start with the mapping of the e-mail activities. On the Fields tab, note that the majority of fields are identical in the source map on the left and the target map on the right. Because you're using the SQL connector, some of the fields are slightly different (this is true across all of the entities) but for the most part match one to one. The mapping of this entity is generally a drag-and-drop exercise. For example, `ActivityId` in the source can be dragged and dropped onto the `activityid` field in the target. We look at two fields in detail: the `ownerid` and the `regardin-gobjecttypecode`. Both require the use of a Scribe Online method and a lookup table. Figure 3-10 shows the mapping of these fields.

**Target: CRM Online Production**

| Name | Type (size) | Formula |
|------|-------------|---------|
| modifiedonbehalfbyyominame | String(4000) | |
| notifications | Integer32 | Email.Notifications |
| notifications_displayname | String(255) | |
| overriddencreatedon | DateTime | Email.CreatedOn |
| ownerid | Guid | LOOKUPTABLEVALUE2_DEFAULT("Owners",Email.OwnerIdName,"EE356F94-6FFD-E211-A47F-B4B52F67D520") |
| owneridname | String(4000) | |
| owneridtype | String(255) | "systemuser" |
| owneridyominame | String(4000) | |
| owningbusinessunit | Guid | |
| owningteam | Guid | |
| owninguser | Guid | |
| prioritycode | Integer32 | Email.PriorityCode |
| prioritycode_displayname | String(255) | |
| readreceiptrequested | Boolean | Email.ReadReceiptRequested |
| regardingobjectid | Guid | Email.RegardingObjectId |
| regardingobjectidname | String(4000) | |
| regardingobjectidyominame | String(4000) | |
| regardingobjecttypecode | String(255) | LOOKUPTABLEVALUE2("EntityCodes",Email.RegardingObjectTypeCode) |

**Figure 3-10.** Mapping the ownerid and regardingobjecttypecode fields

The challenge of mapping `OwnerId` from one environment to another is that the GUIDs most likely will not match. With CRM Online, the users in the target system must be configured and set up differently than on-premise, and this leads to not being able to control the underlying unique identifier for the record. If the GUIDs were identical, you could simply drag and drop the `OwnerId` from the source and drop it on the target, just like all of the other fields. But when the fields are different, you have to go with an alternative solution. One such solution is the use of a Scribe Online lookup table.

A lookup table allows for a key value pair to be configured so that one column is the lookup and the other is the field returned. To configure and call this, take the following steps:

1. Create a new lookup table. Click the Lookup Tables menu option in Scribe Online and click New.

2. Give an appropriate Name and Description.

3. The lookup will be performed on a field that is common between the two environments. This could be done on the e-mail address, name, or other value. For this demonstration, the common field between CRM on-premise and CRM Online will be the full name, available in the `OwnerIdName` in the source data. Set the Value Mappings properties to have the full name of the owner in the Value 1 field, and the CRM Online user GUID in Value 2, as shown in Figure 3-11.

Define two-way value mappings.

**Name** | Owners

Description | Lookup GUID based on full name

**Value Mappings**

➕ NEW    ✕ DELETE

| Value 1 | Value 2 |
|---------|---------|
| Billy Green | 270E71BE-8FED-E211-B7B3-B4B52F566DF2 |
| Johnny Brown | 10D83BB5-A2ED-E211-AB6B-B4B52F67D520 |
| Sally Blue | DEC2A4F0-8FED-E211-B7B3-B4B52F566DF2 |

*Figure 3-11. Owner lookup table*

---

▮ **Note** You can get the GUIDs of the users via several methods from CRM Online. If you happen to have a subscription to Scribe Online Replication Services, simply pull down the user information and write it to a SQL table. If not, you can export the data into a file or pull it down through custom code.

---

Although you will likely find it a tedious process to get all the GUIDs and usernames from Online and to populate a lookup table. For one thing, doing so allows you to keep a simple mapping in Scribe Online. For another, it allows you to filter out and remap the ownership of object that you may want to handle in your migration. For example, say that you have several users in your on-premise environment who are no longer with the company but are still shown as the owner on a number of objects. During the migration, you can map their names to a different (active) user's information in the Online environment.

Another example of a lookup table that you will likely need is for `regarding objecttypecode`. This value in the source data is an integer, yet in the target it is a string. To map this from the source to the target, you need a lookup table. The integer entity codes in the source data all map to a different string representation in the target. The default entities have static codes (for example, `account` is always 1 and `email` is always 4202). Custom entities will have new codes associated with them when they are created. Getting the exact values from CRM Online can be a challenge, unless you have Scribe Online Replication (and can simply pull the data down into a local SQL table) or you have custom .NET code that can retrieve the information. Figure 3-12 shows a lookup table with a number of entity codes and their string value equivalents.

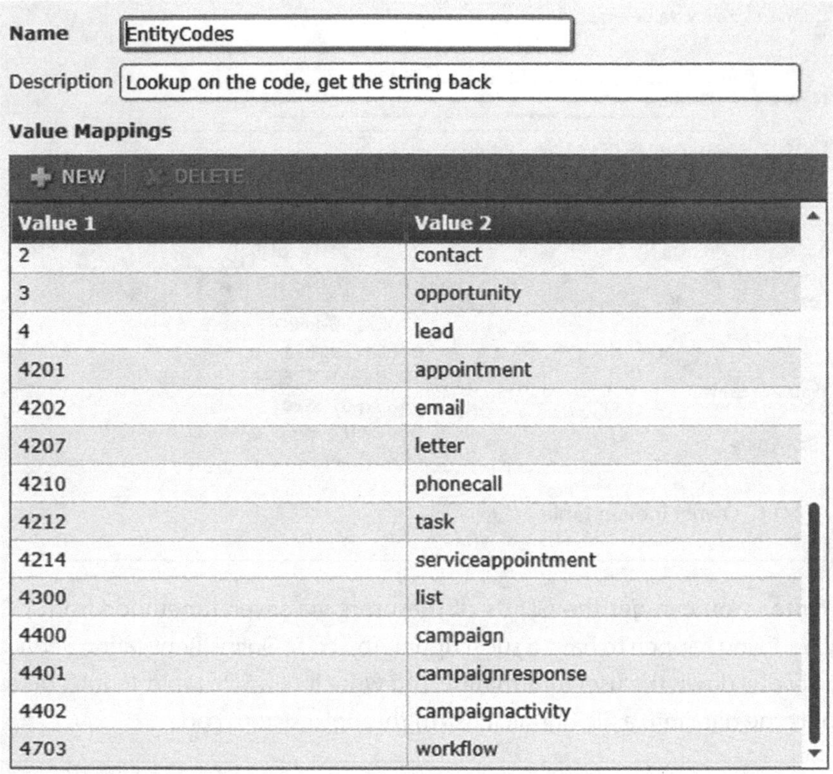

| Name | EntityCodes |
| --- | --- |
| Description | Lookup on the code, get the string back |

**Value Mappings**

+ NEW    ✕ DELETE

| Value 1 | Value 2 |
| --- | --- |
| 2 | contact |
| 3 | opportunity |
| 4 | lead |
| 4201 | appointment |
| 4202 | email |
| 4207 | letter |
| 4210 | phonecall |
| 4212 | task |
| 4214 | serviceappointment |
| 4300 | list |
| 4400 | campaign |
| 4401 | campaignresponse |
| 4402 | campaignactivity |
| 4703 | workflow |

*Figure 3-12. Entity code lookup table*

To call the lookup tables from within a Scribe map, several methods are available. In this case, the owner is being looked up using the LOOKUPTABLEVALUE2_ DEFAULT method, which passes in the name as a string and gets the GUID value back. If no value is found, it defaults to a specific GUID. Here is this method in full:

```
LOOKUPTABLEVALUE2_DEFAULT("Owners",Email.OwnerIdName,
"EE356F94-6FFD-E211-A47F-B4B52F67D520")
```

Calling the entity code lookup table is similar, but the method used is different. It does not return a default value (null is set if the value can't be found). The code for regardingobjecttypecode is shown here:

```
LOOKUPTABLEVALUE2("EntityCodes",
Email.RegardingObjectTypeCode)
```

## Mapping Annotations and File Attachments

Most of the entity mapping you will do is similar to that outlined for the e-mail activities, and you can do most of it using either the SQL Server connector or the Dynamics CRM connector. But there is one data type that can only be migrated using the Dynamics connector: the file attachment, associated with annotations (annotations themselves, without file attachments, can be migrated using either connector). Files are mapped in the `documentbody` field. In CRM this is a byte array, but in SQL it is represented as a string. Figure 3-13 shows the document body field types using the SQL connector on the left and the Dynamics connector on the right. The map has no ability to convert or map these two different types.

| CreatedOnBehalfByYomiName | String(160) | | createdonbehalfbyyominame | String(4000) | |
| DocumentBody | String | | documentbody | Byte Array | |
| FileName | String(255) | | filename | String(255) | Annotation.FileName |

**Figure 3-13.** Document body (attachment) data type descrepancy

To resolve this, you must use the CRM Dynamics connector. As you can see in Figure 3-14, the two data types for the `documentbody` match, and the mapping is a simple drag and drop like other fields. This Mapping will allow the binary data that represents the file attachment to appear correctly in the target CRM Online environment.

| createdonbehalfbyyominame | String(4000) | | createdonbehalfbyyominame | String(4000) | |
| documentbody | Byte Array | | documentbody | Byte Array | annotation.documentbody |
| filename | String(255) | | filename | String(255) | Annotation.FileName |
| filesize | Integer32 | | filesize | Integer32 | |

**Figure 3-14.** `documentbody` matched using Dynamics connector

# Conclusion

This chapter has outlined two of the primary options for migrating and integrating data with CRM. The first is the custom code approach. That is always an option, but it is very labor intensive, prone to errors, and not easy to maintain or reuse. There are cases where you may be required to use a custom approach, but in general you should look for tools and applications that already exist and can be used for your implementation. One of the most appropriate tools for integrations and migrations for CRM is Scribe Online, which has both Integration and Replication Services. By understanding the key concepts to migration and integration, and working through the details presented in this chapter, you should be able to successfully implement your own solution.

# JScript and the REST Endpoint API

## Chapter 4

The REST endpoint API is a service that allows for the querying, updating, and creating of data – all within JScript callable from your CRM forms. In previous versions of CRM, FetchXML could be used to query data, but there were huge limitations on what could be done around updating and creating records. A lot of code had to be written, and the complexities associated with it often resulted in the requirement that a plugin be written. Now, FetchXML is only used for SSRS reporting, while the updating and creating of records is a simple task. This chapter outlines how to work with JScript and web resources, and how to write queries, updates, and creates using the REST endpoint service.

---

■ **Note**  You may hear Jscript called JavaScript. JavaScript and JScript are identical languages with different names. Microsoft has chosen to call it JScript within CRM.

---

## Writing and Triggering JScript

The process of creating a JScript method that can be trigger from an event in CRM is more involved in CRM 2011 than it was in past releases. The process involves creating a web resource, associating it with the appropriate CRM event, and writing the JScript. In order to illustrate the steps required for triggering JScript, start with a simple method stub.

For the purposes of this chapter, the method will be called getCurrentUser, and for now it will have a single alert within it, so that you can easily tell if it is being called successfully or not. The simple starter method is shown in Listing 4-1. It will be triggered on the OnLoad event of a CRM form.

*Listing 4-1.* Simple JScript Method

```
function getCurrentUser()
{
 alert("test");
}
```

## Create a Web Resource

All JScript used within CRM must be contained in a Web Resource. There are a variety of web resource types, one of which is Jscript. The first step is to click New in Web Resources within the Customization Settings menu of CRM (see Figure 4-1). You will need to give it an appropriate name and set the type to Script (JScript). You can paste the code from Listing 4-1 in the screen that pops up when you click the Text Editor button.

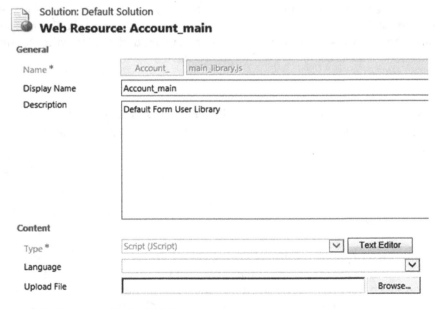

**Figure 4-1.** Creating a JScript Web Resource

Once you have created this, click Publish All Customizations to make this available to reference from within CRM Forms.

> **Note** Work to make your JScript web resource files as reusable as possible. For example, you may have a requirement to format phone numbers that are entered in multiple fields in the account, contact, and lead entity forms. Instead of creating one web resource for each entity (or worse, one method for each phone number field on each entity), create a single generic web resource that is called something like "Utilities" and can be referenced in multiple locations. You don't want to have massive JScript files, but you also want to make your code as reusable as you can, and follow standard coding best practices.

## Reference the Web Resource

The next step is to reference the Web Resource you just created from within a CRM Form. To add the web resource and call the method during the OnLoad event of a form, open a form to customize it and click on the Form Properties button. In the Form Properties window that opens, click Add under the Form Libraries. This will allow you to reference the form(s) that have methods that you want to call.

With the web resource added to the form library, you can now set the event that will trigger the call to the method. In this case, in the Event Handlers section, set the Control property to Form, the Event property to OnLoad, and click the Add button.

On the Handler Properties window, set the Library equal to the web resource library, and set the Function property equal to the name of your method (no parenthesis required). In this case, it will be set to getCurrentUser. Make sure that the Enabled field is set. Figure 4-2 shows the required settings on the various windows.

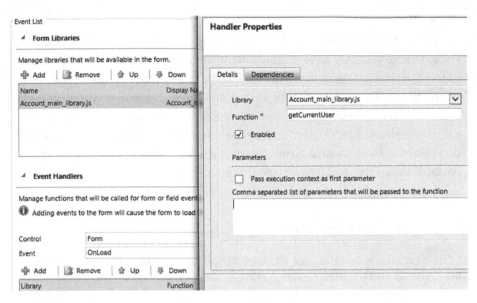

**Figure 4-2.** Referencing the JScript Method and Library from the Form

Once the properties have been set as described, you will need to save everything and click on the Publish button (or Publish All Customizations, depending on which screen you are on). With everything published, the alert should pop up the moment you open the Account form in CRM.

> ■ **Note** Once you have the initial JScript method working and validated from your trigger event, you can continue to update and test the code by doing only two of the steps outlined in this section – modify the code in the web reference and click the Publish button.

Using a simple method with nothing more than a call to alert() is helpful to ensure that you are able to reference and call your JScript from within a form event – but once you have this simple code working, you will want to extend it with real world solutions. In the next section, you'll look at ways in which to query data using OData and populate fields on your form with the results.

## Incorporating OData/REST Queries

OData is a greatly improved and simplified approach to querying data that is new to CRM 2011. The OData queries are run through a single WCF service available in CRM – OrganizationData.svc. While previous options for querying data from JScript are still supported (at least for the time being), OData is the approach you will want to take for any new development. OData allows for access to data without extensive coding and with a standard pattern for all entities.

Before you can add OData queries to your JScript, you will need to add an additional web resource to your list. This script that must be added is json2.js, and can be found in the CRM SDK. Once you have added this as a new web resource, you will need to add it to the list of libraries available on the form that you are working with (steps for doing both of these steps are outlined earlier in this chapter). Figure 4-3 shows this referenced library.

**Form Properties**
Modify this form's properties.

| Events | Display | Parameters | Non-Event Dependencies |

**Event List**

◢ **Form Libraries**

Manage libraries that will be available in the form.

➕ Add | 📝 Remove | ⬆ Up | ⬇ Down | 📝 Edit

| Name | Display Name | Description |
|------|--------------|-------------|
| Account_main_library.js | Account_main | Default Form User Lib... |
| new_json2.js | json2 | |

**Figure 4-3.** Required JSON Library File

■ **Note** The CRM SDK can be downloaded at http://www.microsoft.com/en-us/download/details.aspx?id=24004. Scripts (including the json2.js file) can be found in sdk\samplecode\js\restendpoint\javascriptrestdataoperations\javascriptrestdataoperations\scripts.

## OData Queries with Single Results

Listing 4-2 uses the same getCurrentUser() method that was built earlier in this chapter, but adds code to set the value of a field on the form to the first and last name of the current user. This is an example of querying a simple type – the response is a string on a single result, and there is no need to loop through the results in order to work with the data.

*Listing 4-2.* Querying the System User Entity with OData

```
function getCurrentUser()
{
 var currentUserID = Xrm.Page.context.getUserId();
 if(currentUserID != null)
 {
  var serverUrl = Xrm.Page.context.getServerUrl();

  var oDataEndpointUrl = serverUrl +"/XrmServices/2011/
OrganizationData.svc/";
  oDataEndpointUrl +=
   "SystemUserSet?$select=SystemUserId,FullName&$filter=
SystemUserId eq (guid'" + currentUserID + "')";

  var service = new ActiveXObject("MSXML2.XMLHTTP.3.0");

  if(ser vice != null)
  {
   service.open("Get",oDataEndpointUrl,false);
   service.setRequestHeader("X-Requested-
Width","XMLHttpRequest");
   service.SetRequestHeader("Accept","application/json,
text/javascript, */*");
   service.send(null);

   var requestResults = eval('('+service.responseText +')')
.d.results;

   if(requestResults != null && requestResults.length >= 1)
   {
    var userEntity = requestResults[0];
    var result = null;
    var id = userEntity.SystemUserId;
    var Name = userEntity.FullName;
    Xrm.Page.getAttribute("new_username").setValue(Name);
   }
  }
 }
}
```

The critical aspects of this code are as follows:

1. Xrm.Page.context.getUserId(). This method will get the current user's system user GUID. This value will be used as a parameter in the lookup of the user's data.

2. Xrm.Page.context.getServerUrl(). This will get the current URL of the environment the code is executing within. This approach ensures that as you move your code between environments, the changing URLs will always be accessed correctly.

3. The OData Endpoint URL. There are several lines dedicated to setting the URL and parameters for the OData query. The portion you will be altering depending on the data you are querying is everything that is set within the oDataEndPointUrl field (found after the OrganizationData.svc declaration in the URL). The entity you are querying and the filter on the data you are after is all set within this URL.

4. The instantiation and call of the OData service. There are a number of lines of code used to open and call the web service for the data. This code is identical for every service call.

5. Getting the results. In this case, a single result (or no result) will always be returned – there will never be multiple records in the result. Therefore, the data can be retrieved directly from the first element of the results and translated into a string that can be used to populate a field.

6. Xrm.Page.getAttribute("new_username").setValue(Name). This code will set the value of the new_username field on the form to the result that was returned.

## OData Queries with Multiple Results

Frequently, you will need to query data that returns more than a single record, and then loop through the results in order to perform logic or populate fields within your form. Listing 4-3 shows how to query the account entity for all inactive records, and how to loop through the results to get access to the data within.

*Listing 4-3.* Querying the Account Entity with OData

```
function getInactiveAccounts()
{
 var serverUrl = Xrm.Page.context.getServerUrl();

 var oDataEndpointUrl = serverUrl +"/XrmServices/2011/
OrganizationData.svc/";
```

```
oDataEndpointUrl += "AccountSet?$select=Name&$filter=
StateCode/Value eq 1";

var service = new ActiveXObject("MSXML2.XMLHTTP.3.0");

if(service != null)
{
  service.open("Get",oDataEndpointUrl,false);
  service.setRequestHeader("X-Requested-
Width","XMLHttpRequest");
  service.SetRequestHeader("Accept","application/json,
text/javascript, */*");
  service.send(null);

  var requestResults = eval('('+service.responseText +')')
.d.results;

  if(requestResults != null && requestResults.length >= 1)
  {
   for(var i = 0;i<requestResults.length;i++)
   {
    var accountEntity = requestResults[i];
    alert(accountEntity.Name);
   }
  }
}
```

The most important portions of this code are as follows:

1.  The service instantiation. Notice that the service code is identical to the previous single result code (Listing 4-2). Realize that once you have written this, the parameters to the URL are the only dynamic section you have to deal with for the various queries you will need to perform.

2.  The OData Endpoint URL. Here, you can see that the Account entity is being queried. The Name field is being returned and the filter is based on the state of the record being inactive.

3.  For Loop. This loop shows how to grab values in the array that is returned. Any values that you have in the select statement in your query will be available in the result object within this loop (in this case, only the Name field is available).

### Anatomy of an OData Query

When building the URL parameters for the OData query, there are a variety of options available. The query syntax is made up of the entity being queried and the query options (select, filter, order by, etc.) One of the easiest ways to think of the syntax is in terms of standard T-SQL. For example, the query from Listing 4-3 that pulls data from the account record is as follows:

```
AccountSet?$select=Name&$filter=StateCode/Value eq 1
```

Writing this in T-SQL gives the following:

```
SELECT Name
FROM Account
WHERE StateCode = 1
```

Extending the OData query to pull back multiple columns can be done in a comma separated list, while supporting additional filters can be added by separating each with a directive such as with an AND or an OR operator. An example of the T-SQL and the identical OData query are shown here:

```
SELECT Name
     ,new_startdate
     ,new_category
FROM Account
WHERE StateCode = 1
AND new_category = 'Finance'
```

```
AccountSet?$select=Name,new_startdate,new_
category&$filter=StateCode/Value eq 1 and new_category eq
'Finance'
```

The name of the entity being queried is always retrieved from the schema name of the entity, which is available from the entity list in the Customization menu in Settings (as shown in the highlighted column in Figure 4-4).

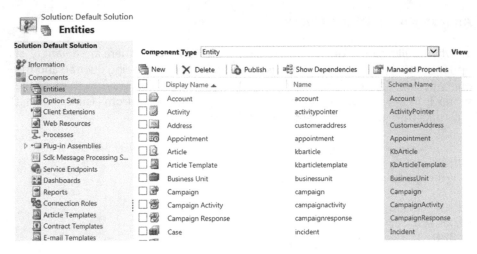

**Figure 4-4.** The Schema Name used for OData queries

There are several query options beyond the $select and $filter, many of which are shown in Table 4-1.

**Table 4-1.** Query Options

| Query Option | Description |
|---|---|
| $expand | Similar to a JOIN in T-SQL, the $expand option will add in related entities to the query. Once the related entities are defined, you can pull back their fields in the $select list, along with the parent entity defined. The maximum number of related entities is currently limited to six. |
| $filter | This is the list of filters that are set on the query. This is similar to T-SQL (though not as robust). |
| $orderby | You can order the result set that is returned by including this query option. Standard T-SQL syntax applies here (for example, ascending is ASC and descending is DESC). |
| $select | The $select query option is the list of fields that are going to be brought back in the query result set. |
| $top | Using the $top query option will limit the total number of results that are returned. |

An example of the earlier OData query with several more of the query options in Table 4-1 applied is shown here:

```
AccountSet?$select=Name,new_startdate,new_
category&$orderby=new_startdate
desc&$top=10&$filter=StateCode/Value eq 1 and new_
category eq 'Finance'
```

The T-SQL for this is:

```
SELECT TOP 10 Name
     ,new_startdate
     ,new_category
FROM Account
WHERE StateCode = 1
AND new_category = 'Finance'
ORDER BY new_startdate DESC
```

> **Note** There is a great tool available from CodePlex that helps with the construction of OData queries – the OData Query Designer. It is available for download from `https://crm2011odatatool.codeplex.com`.

There is quite a bit of flexibility in how you create your OData queries, and the query support is fairly robust. You certainly don't have the ability to build complex queries available in full T-SQL, but with some creativity and thought, you will be able to retrieve the data you are after – all from JScript within your CRM Form.

## Creating and Updating Records with OData/REST

Not only can you query data using the REST endpoints, but you can also create and update records. The ability to have this level of control within JScript is enormously powerful. The update and create processes are very similar in syntax. Both start with creating a list of attributes that will be added/updated to the entity record, and then pass this array of attributes into the REST service.

### Update Record

Looking first at the update of an existing record, the first step is to get the GUID of the entity record that you will be updating. There are a variety of options for this, depending on what fields you have available to you within the form. One option would be to grab the GUID from a lookup field that is on the CRM form. Another option would be to get the GUID from an OData query (as outlined earlier in this chapter). This code will assume that you have access to a GUID, and will place this value into a variable called "id".

```
var id ="D2CA7A4C-D105-E311-A5D1-B4B52F67D694";
```

The next step is to create an array that holds the attribute names and the corresponding values associated with these attributes. This array should contain all of the attribute/value pairs that you want to update in the target record. For purposes of illustration, these values will be hardcoded into the array, but in a real world scenario, you would likely be grabbing these either from separate OData queries, or from fields within your CRM Form.

```
var updateVals=["new_address1,new_City,new_State ",
"23 A Lane,Boulder,CO"];
```

With the data in the array, you can now build out the service instantiation code and pass this array into it. The service instantiation is very similar to what you have already looked at for querying data, but does have several setRequstHeader directives that must be included. There is one unique to an update, that neither the query nor the create methods use, which is:

```
service.setRequestHeader("X-HTTP-Method","MERGE");
```

When the service is instantiated, the state of the process must be listened for, and cannot be written to until it is in a certain status. Listening for this state is shown here:

```
service.onreadystatechange = function(){
 if(this.readyState == 4)
```

The full code for an update is shown in Listing 4-4.

*Listing 4-4.* Update Method

```
function UpdateRecord()
{
 var id ="D2CA7A4C-D105-E311-A5D1-B4B52F67D694";
 var updateVals=["new_address1,new_City,new_State ",
"23 A Lane,Boulder,CO"];
 var strEntitySet ="AccountSet";

 // assign the fields and values to the array
 var array=[];
 for(var i = 0;i < updateVals.length;i++)
 {
  array[i] = updateVals[i].split(",");
 }

 var entity = new Object();
 for(var i = 0;i < 1;i++)
 {
  for(var j = 0;j < array[i].length;j++)
```

```
  {
    entity[[array[i][j]]]=array[i + 1][j];
  }
}

 var serverUrl = Xrm.Page.context.getServerUrl();
 var service = new ActiveXObject("MSXML2.XMLHTTP.3.0");
 var oDataEndpointUrl = serverUrl +"/XrmServices/2011/
OrganizationData.svc/";
 oDataEndpointUrl += strEntitySet;
 oDataEndpointUrl += "(guid'"+id+"')";

 service.open("POST",encodeURI(oDataEndpointUrl),true);
 service.setRequestHeader("Accept","application/json");
 service.setRequestHeader("Content-Type","application/
json; charset=utf-8");
 service.setRequestHeader("X-HTTP-Method","MERGE");
 service.onreadystatechange = function(){
 if(this.readyState == 4)
 {
   if(this.status==204||this.status==1223)
   {}
   else
   {
     ErrorHandler(service);
   }
 }
};
service.send(JSON.stringify(entity));
}
```

## Create Record

The creation of a record uses code that is almost identical to what is used for the update of a record. The primary differences are:

1.  You do not need to specify a GUID – this will be automatically created by CRM.

2.  You do not need to set the request header for ("X-HTTP-Method", "MERGE").

3.  You must pass in any required fields. In the update, you created an array of fields that needed to be updated – this could be any list of fields desired. But with the call to create a record, the list of fields must – at a minimum – contain all of the fields required on the creation of a record.

## Conclusion

This chapter has outlined how to create JScript web resources and reference them from within your CRM forms, and trigger them off of events. It has also looked at querying, creating, and updating data from within JScript using the REST endpoints (also known as OData queries). This functionality is immensely valuable, and allows for virtually any kind of data querying and manipulation needed – all within the JScript of a form. With little coding required, you can work through the REST endpoint API and accomplish tasks that previously could only be handled through C# and plugins.

# Reporting

## Chapter 5

This chapter outlines how to build SSRS reports that are hosted in CRM Online. CRM on-premise has a database, and SSRS reports can be built using standard SQL queries. CRM Online, however, does not have a database that is accessible to end users, and therefore all reporting must be done through the CRM API. Developing SQL Server Report Services (SSRS) reports using this API requires a shift in thinking around how best to solve reporting requirements that wouldn't take a second thought when developing directly against SQL Server. This chapter will outline how to set up SSRS, how to connect to CRM Online, and how to build SSRS reports in order to query and display data from CRM Online.

## SSRS Development Environment

As the MSDN documentation states:

"For security reasons, you cannot deploy custom SQL-based reports to Microsoft Dynamics CRM Online."

This creates a challenge for SSRS developers – if you can't write SQL in SQL Server Report Services, then how can you query the data? Microsoft's solution is FetchXML, and they have provided a toolkit called the Dynamics CRM Report Authoring Extension, which is an add-on to the Business Intelligence Development Studio (BIDS). In order to write custom reports for CRM Online, take these steps:

1. Ensure that BIDS is available on your development machine. BIDS is a default installation with any SQL Server install, so if you have SQL Server on your machine, you should see SQL Server Business Intelligence Development Studio. This runs within the Visual Studio shell.

2. Install the Dynamics CRM Report Authoring Extension, available at `http://www.microsoft.com/en-us/download/details.aspx?id=27823.`

## Creating a Report Project and Report

Once your development environment is fully installed, you will be able to create a new project for developing your reports. Click on File ➤ New ➤ Project and select the Report Server Project from the Business Intelligence Projects, as shown in Figure 5-1. Name the project appropriately and click OK. This will create a new project where you can add data sources, datasets, and reports.

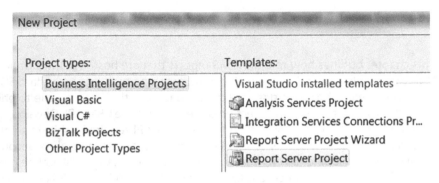

**Figure 5-1.** Creating a new Report Server Project

Once the project has been created, you can create a new report by right clicking Reports and selecting Add New Report. This will open the Report Wizard. You can click through the wizard to create a report template to work from. You can also download a report from CRM Online that is already formatted with the look and feel you want, and use that as a starting point. Look for a report that uses Microsoft Dynamics CRM Fetch as the data source, as outlined in the next section.

---

■ **Note**   In the chapter on Integration and Migration (Chapter 3), Scribe Online was discussed in detail.  One of the tools available is replication, which allows you to pull down data from a CRM environment to a local SQL database.  In the case of CRM Online, it will pull down all of the data and create a default set of tables in SQL that closely resemble the table structures of CRM on-premise installs.  For reporting, you may decide that you want to build some SSRS reports outside of CRM and host them locally.  In this case, you can pull data directly from these SQL tables and display via traditional means in SSRS.

---

## Connecting to CRM Online from SSRS

BIDS now has an option to use Microsoft Dynamics CRM Fetch as a data source. In order to access this, open a report and open (or create) the data source shown under Data Sources in the Report Data window, as shown in Figure 5-2.

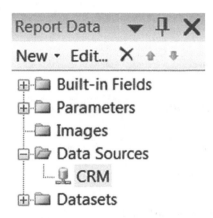

**Figure 5-2.** Data Sources in the Report Data Window

Once the data source window is open, you will be able to configure the connection. Take the following steps to complete a connection. Figure 5-3 shows a fully functional configuration.

1. Give the data source a descriptive name.

2. Select Embedded connection.

3. Set the Type property to Microsoft Dynamics CRM Fetch.

4. Set the connection string using the following pattern: `https://[organization].crm.dynamics.com/;[organization];`

---

■ **Note**  You will be able to get the exact organization name and URL pattern through your CRM Online solution. Click on Settings and select Developer Resources from the Customization tab. The Organization Unique Name will give you the organization name, and the first part of the Organization Data Service URL (everything before the XRMServices path) will give you the correct URL pattern.

---

5. Under the Credentials tab, select the Use this name and password option and enter in your Office 365 credentials.

6. Click OK to save your settings. You will be able to test out connectivity once you create a dataset.

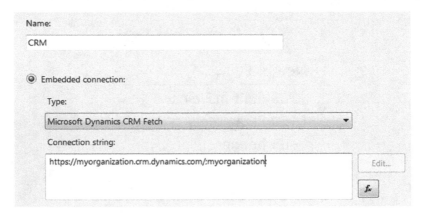

**Figure 5-3.** Data Source Connection String

## Querying and Displaying Data

Now that you have created a data source connection, you can build a dataset to query CRM Online. Using the Report Data window, right click Datasets and select Add Dataset (or open an existing dataset, if you are starting from an existing report). To start with, you will create a simple query by opening an Advanced Find window in CRM Online and setting the query to something similar to that shown in Figure 5-4. Your simple query should filter on something meaningful within an entity that you want to work with.

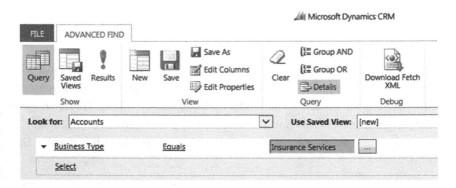

**Figure 5-4.** Sample Advanced Find

With the query defined, click the Edit Columns button and add the columns that you want to display in your report. The default view will only show certain columns, and you'll likely want more fields. This is not a requirement, but it does make it easier to get the field names here, rather than having to look them up on the entity forms/fields later.

Once you have the query and the fields ready, click the Download Fetch XML button. This will open the XML in a new window. Right click and select View Source so that you can copy this easily and then paste it into your Query Text, as shown in Figure 5-5. Clicking the Refresh Fields button will force a connection to CRM Online, and will validate both your dataset and your data source. If there are any issues with your query or with your connection string and credentials, you will get an error (which you will need to address).

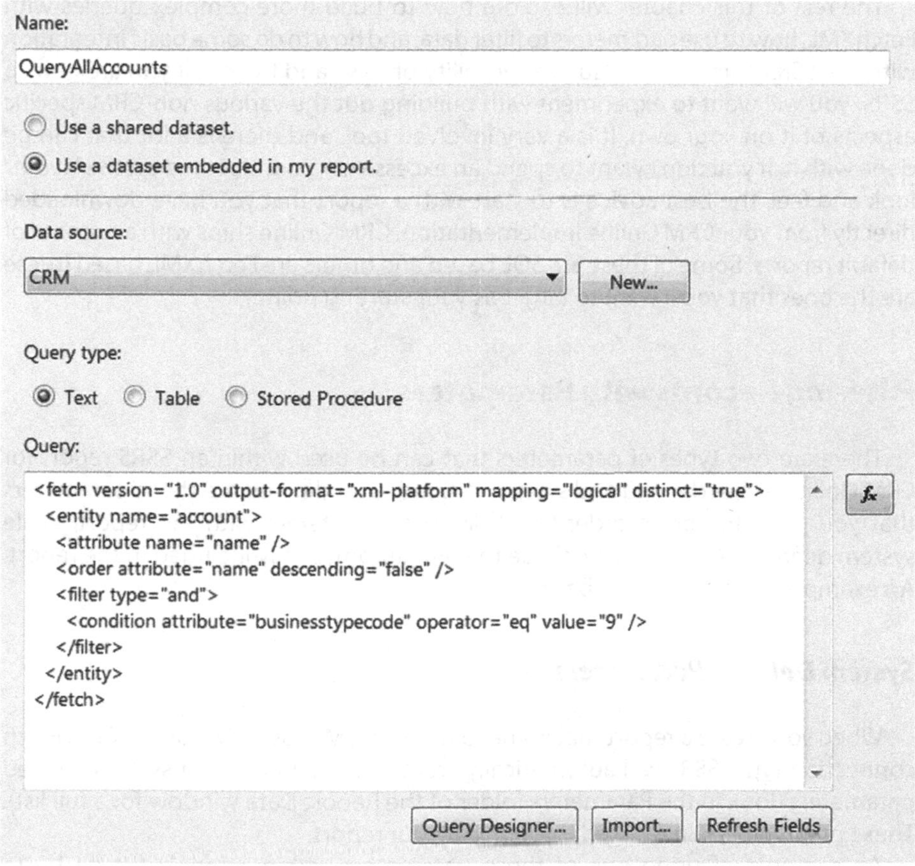

Name:

QueryAllAccounts

○ Use a shared dataset.
◉ Use a dataset embedded in my report.

Data source:

CRM ▼    New...

Query type:

◉ Text    ○ Table    ○ Stored Procedure

Query:

```
<fetch version="1.0" output-format="xml-platform" mapping="logical" distinct="true">
  <entity name="account">
   <attribute name="name" />
   <order attribute="name" descending="false" />
   <filter type="and">
    <condition attribute="businesstypecode" operator="eq" value="9" />
   </filter>
  </entity>
</fetch>
```

Query Designer...    Import...    Refresh Fields

Figure 5-5. Query Text in the Dataset

> **Note** Using the Advanced Find is a great starting point to getting the FetchXML that you need. However, it will not let you create intricate relationships (joins) that you will likely want within your reports. The Advanced Find interface is limited to one level child relationships, whereas you can build any hierarchy you want within SSRS FetchXML.

The next step is to display your data in a table in your report. In the Tablix properties of your table, set the Dataset name to the dataset that you created. This will bind the table to your dataset, and force it to display results when you run your report. You can click the Preview tab to view the final product.

The rest of this chapter will explore how to build more complex queries with FetchXML, how to use parameters to filter data, and how to do some basic integration with the SSRS components (such as visibility of rows and tables). If you are new to SSRS, you will want to experiment with building out the various non-CRM specific aspects of it on your own. It is a very involved tool, and there is a lot that can be done with it. If you don't want to spend an excessive amount of time on the layout/look and feel, the best advice is to start with a report that you have downloaded directly from your CRM Online implementation. CRM Online ships with a number of default reports. Some of these are SQL based and others are FetchXML based (these are the ones that you'll want to target as your starting point.)

## Filtering Records with Parameters

There are two types of parameters that can be used within an SSRS report for CRM Online – user defined and system defined. User defined are those parameters that you need to add in order to allow users to interact with the report, while system defined parameters are those that are automatically included in the report. An example of both will now be shown.

### *System Defined Parameters*

When you create a report that is linked using the Microsoft Dynamics CRM Fetch connection type, SSRS will automatically create a large number of system defined parameters (look in the Parameters folder of the Report Data window for a full list). These parameters can be used throughout your report.

An example of using one of these parameters within a report would be to add the current user's full name to the report title. In the list of system generated parameters, you will see CRM_FullName. Adding this to the title can be done as shown in Figure 5-6.

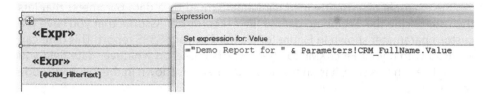

**Figure 5-6.** Using the CRM_FullName Parameter in the Report Title

One of the most useful of the system defined parameters doesn't actually show as a specific parameter within the Parameters folder, but is available behind the scenes. This is the current user's unique identifier (which maps to the systemuser entity in CRM). This field can be used to filter results based on whoever the current user is that is running the report from within the context of CRM.

For example, say that you want to return records that are owned by the current user. You can add a filter to your FetchXML that limits the results to the user that is currently running the report. An example of extending the query shown in Figure 5-5 earlier in this chapter is shown in Listing 5-1. The eq-userid directive gets the current user's id from the context of the running report and compares it with the ownerid of the account record. You can use this filtering approach on any field (not just ownerid) that links to a user on any record.

*Listing 5-1.* Filtering Accounts on Current User

```
<fetch version="1.0" output-format="xml-platform"
mapping="logical"
distinct="true">
 <entity name="account">
  <attribute name="name" />
  <order attribute="name" descending="false" />
  <filter type="and">
   <condition attribute="businesstypecode" operator="eq"
value="9" />
   <condition attribute="ownerid" operator="eq-userid" />
  </filter>
 </entity>
</fetch>
```

## User Defined Parameters

Frequently, you will want to create custom parameters to allow for additional filtering within your FetchXML. You can create custom parameters within SSRS by right clicking the Parameters folder and selecting Add Parameter. You can create a variety of parameters of varying types, and with whatever values you want, queried, hardcoded, or otherwise.

One example of a user defined parameter would be a date parameter that lets the user decide the beginning date to filter records on. Assume that you have the custom parameter shown in Figure 5-7 defined in your SSRS report. This date can be used within your FetchXML to filter records based on whatever date field you would like – in this case, it is on the new_date field, as shown in the following code segment:

```
<filter type="and">
 <condition attribute="new_date" operator="on-or-after"
value="@StartDate"/>
</filter>
```

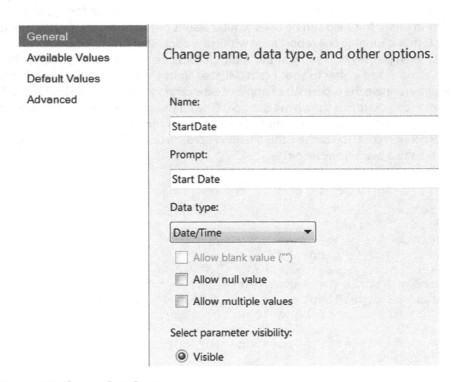

**Figure 5-7.** Custom Date Parameter

---

■ **Note**   In order for custom parameters to be used within your FetchXML, you will need to make sure the Parameters tab on the Dataset properties maps the parameter which is defined in the Parameters folder to the name of the custom parameter in the FetchXML, as shown in Figure 5-8.

---

**Figure 5-8.** The Parameters Tab on the Dataset Properties

## Linking Child Records

In many cases, you will want to create reports that show data from a variety of records. This section will demonstrate how to show several levels of child records and linked records.

All linking within FetchXML (which is handled through the link-entity node) is similar to joins within SQL queries. You can think of CRM entities like SQL tables, where the top level table can get data from related tables by joining on specific common fields. In the case of FetchXML, there are some serious limitations when compared with SQL, but if you are creative, you can usually figure out something that will match almost exactly what you can do through standard SQL queries.

For purposes of illustration, assume that you have a top level entity called Lease, and you want to show records from several child entities. Leases have Lease Contacts, and Lease Contacts are linked to actual Contact records. Leases also have Buildings. You want to show data from all of these records within a single row in your SSRS report table. The code shown in Listing 5-2 demonstrates how to pull records from the various entities.

*Listing 5-2.* Working with Linked Entities

```
<fetch version="1.0" output-format="xml-platform"
mapping="logical"
distinct="true">
 <entity name="new_lease">
  <attribute name="new_name" />
  <filter type="and">
   <condition attribute="statuscode" value="1"
operator="eq"/>
   <condition attribute="statecode" value="0"
operator="eq"/>
  </filter>
  <order attribute="new_name" descending="false" />
  <link-entity name="new_leasecontacts"
```

```
from="new_leaseid" to="new_leaseid"
  alias="lc" link-type="outer">
   <attribute name="new_name" />
   <attribute name="new_contacttype" />
   <link-entity name="contact" from="contactid"
to="new_contactid" alias="c"
   link-type="outer">
    <attribute name="fullname" />
    <attribute name="emailaddress1" />
   </link-entity>
  </link-entity>
  <link-entity name="new_building" from="new_buildingid"
to="new_buildingid"
   alias="complex" link-type="outer">
   <attribute name="ownerid" />
  </link-entity>
 </entity>
</fetch>
```

One key item to note here is the link-type attribute – in this listing it is set to "outer", which means all records will be returned at all levels. In this case, it will return all leases, whether their lease contact has an email address or not. If you leave this attribute out, the results will be limited to leases that have contacts with email addresses.

## Additional Filtering in SSRS

With FetchXML, you will find that there are often times when you cannot filter all of the data in the exact way that you would like. In those cases, you may need to bring back a superset of data and further filter it once it is inside of the report itself. One way to do this is to tie all of the results to a table (as usual), but set the visibility of the row displayed to a formula that filters out the additional data that you do not want displayed.

In order to set the visibility on a row, right click the row within the table control and select Row Visibility. You will see a property that is available titled "Show or hide based on an expression" (See Figure 5-9). This property allows code to be written that will determine whether to show the data or not. The following two example will illustrate the use of the expression shape for setting visibility.

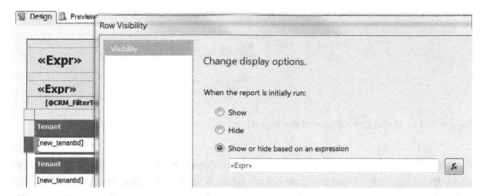

**Figure 5-9.** Setting an Expression for Row Visibility

In this example, the requirement is to only show the record if the month of the date in the row matches the month selected in a user defined parameter in the report. The parameter (in this case title Months) has the twelve months set in string equivalents in the parameter definition, as shown in Figure 5-10. Figure 5-11 shows this date parameter on the deployed report in action.

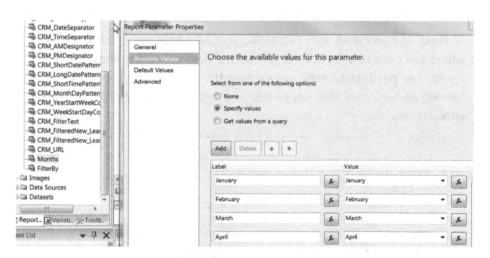

**Figure 5-10.** User Defined Parameter for Months

**Figure 5-11.** In the Drop Down of the Report

With the user defined property configured, the visibility expression is set to only show those records where the date equals what is selected, as shown in the following code. This uses several built in functions available in SSRS – the Month (which gets the numeric representation of the month from the new_anniversarydate field) and the MonthName (which converts the numeric value into a string representation of a date) and then compares it with the string value selected in the parameter.

```
=IIF(MonthName(Month(Fields!account_new_anniversarydate
.Value)) =
Parameters!Months.Value,False,True)
```

> **Note** As you work with FetchXML, you will likely come across scenarios where you need to pull back multiple sets of data in order to filter and get the results you need. Make sure and explore the value of the Lookup methods (see Figure 5-12) that SSRS has so that you can work with your data in a more effective way.

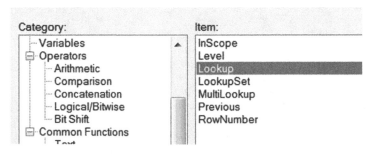

**Figure 5-12.** Advanced Methods Available in SSRS, Useful for Filtering

## Conclusion

This chapter has gone into detail about how to use the CRM API's FetchXML for reporting. You will want to ensure that you explore all of the capabilities of SSRS and report creation and logic, but at this point, you should have all of the information needed to create your own custom reports, and to be successful with building out more complex queries. In earlier versions of CRM, FetchXML was used extensively to query data in multiple areas – plugins (C#), JavaScript, etc. Now, it is used almost exclusively by SSRS reports.

# Index

# O

OData/REST query
  anatomy
    AND/OR operator, 55
    $expand option, 56
    $filter, 56
    $orderby, 56
    schema name, 55–56
    $select option, 56
    standard T-SQL, 55
    $top option, 56
    URL parameters, 55
  JSON library file, 51
  multiple results, 53
  record creation, 59
  single results, 52
  update record, 57

# P, Q, R

Plugins
  debug (see Debugging plugins)
  development
    code framework, 1
    core functionality, 3, 6
    data query, 3
    e-mail, 4
    setting state, 4
  registration
    assembly, 10
    event handler and name, 13
    eventing pipeline stage, 13
    execution mode, 13
    potential events, 13
    primary entity, 13
    tool, 9
    user's context, 13

# S, T

Scribe Online
  annotation/attachment
    migration, 40–41, 45
  connection type options, 35

Dynamics Online connection, 38–39
Dynamics on-premise connection, 37, 39
e-mail activity migration, 40
integration services solution, 38
lookup table, 42
mapping email activity, 41
on-premise agent, 33
SQL Server connection, 35–36, 39
SQL Server Report Services (SSRS) reports
  advanced methods, 72
  child and linked records, 69
  CRM online, 63
  development, 61
  parameters
    date parameter, 71
    system defined parameter, 66
    user defined parameter, 67, 71
    visibility expression, 71
  query and display data, 64
  report server project, 62
System defined parameters, 66

# U, V

User defined parameter, 67, 71

# W

Workflow activity
  development, 7
  registration
    assembly, 10
    event handler and name, 13
    eventing pipeline stage, 13
    execution mode, 13
    potential events, 13
    primary entity, 13
    tool, 9
    user's context, 13

# X, Y, Z

Xrm.Page.context.getServerUrl() method, 53
Xrm.Page.context.getUserId() method, 53